Endpapers: the 17-storey atrium that forms the heart of the James R Thompson Center, Chicago, 1985, by Helmut Jahn, is surmounted by a diagonally-truncated glass cylinder

MODERN ARCHITECTURE

Facing page: *Beurs World Trade Centre, Rotterdam, 1984–87*

CHAUCER PRESS
LONDON

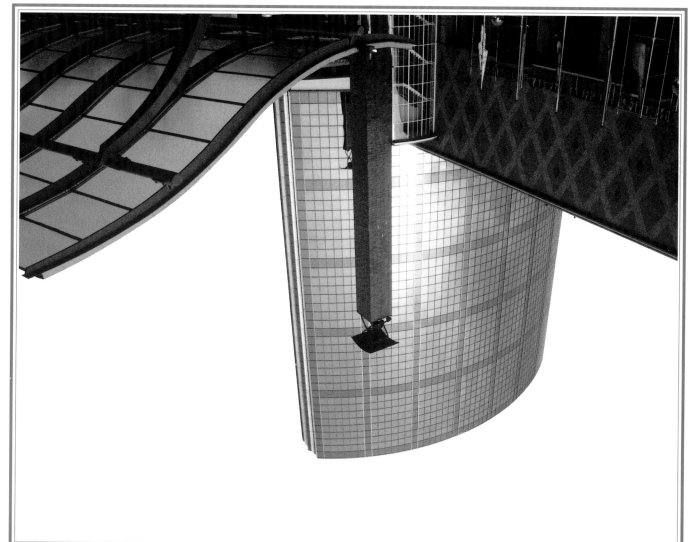

MODERN ARCHITECTURE

First published in Great Britain by
Chaucer Press
an imprint of the
Caxton Publishing Group
20 Bloomsbury Street
London WC1B 3JH

ISBN 1 904449 03 4

Designed and produced by Superlaunch Ltd
P.O. Box 207, Abingdon
Oxfordshire OX13 6TA
Imagesetting and colour reproduction by
International Graphic Services, Bath
Printed and bound in China by
Sun Fung Offset Binding Company Limited

Contents

Chapter One

An Appraisal of Modern Architecture

The 1920s

THE EDWARDIAN PERIOD OF ARCHITECTURE, which is generally considered to have have continued until the outbreak of the First World War in 1914, saw a rich and varied pluralism of style, with a *beaux-arts* classicism extending its influence across Europe but most noticeably in France, the United States and England. Pockets of medieval revivalism continued in England also, alongside strands of national romanticism linked to the Arts and Crafts movement and to regionalist ideals.

After the War, from about 1920, the various strands of modern architecture tended to converge, culminating in the broad international style and the formation of the principles which controlled the modern movement in architecture for the two decades before the Second World War.

Facing page: *our timespan is seen in Chicago's skyline; from left to right, the Jeweller's Building, 1924–26, Union Insurance offices, 1962, Leo Burnett Building, 1989, and the R R Donnelley Building, 1992*

Below: beaux-arts *in France around 1900, at its most varied in the Atlantic coastal town of Mers-les-Bains, where local architects such as J Dupont and A Lasnel were prolific*

Le Corbusier: the early years

Le Corbusier exhibited two projects at the *Salon d'Automne* in 1922, expressing his idea of social environment and thus containing the germ of all contemporary works. The Citrohan House shows all five elements central to his conception of modern architecture: pillars to support the structure; a roof terrace; an open floor plan; a façade free of ornamentation, and windows in strips denoting the independence of the structural frame.

His ideas for city planning were defined at the *Salon d'Automne* and developed for the 1925 *Exposition des Arts Décoratifs*, Paris, in a pavilion that was to be a 'manifesto of the *esprit nouveau*'.

His social ideals were realised twice between 1922 and 1939; first in the workers' city of 40 houses at Pessac, near Bordeaux, 1925–26, that he built in the style of the Citrohan House, and again in 1927, when he participated in the international exposition of the Deutscher Werkbund, for which he built two houses in the experimental residential quarter of Weissenhof, Stuttgart.

Although Le Corbusier was always interested in building for large numbers of people, during the prewar period he built primarily for those who could commission individual houses. These were functional in design and aescetic in appearance, incorporating rigorous geometric forms and bare façades, the prime examples of which are detailed within the main text.

Above right: *Villas La Roche and Jenneret, 8 and 10 Sq du Docteur-Blanche, Auteuil, Paris, 1923, by Le Corbusier; now the Corbusier Museum, 55 rue du Docteur-Blanche. The buildings were not only raised on stilts but also demonstrated the other stylistic characteristics that Le Corbusier initially brought to house design*

So marked was this consolidation, that Charles-Édouard Jeanneret-Gris (Le Corbusier) was able to evaluate the basic principles in just five 'free' characteristics; the freeing of the ground floor by the introduction of freestanding supports; the independence of the structural skeleton of a building from the wall surfaces; the free plan; the free design of the façade; and the introduction of the free level on the roof.

Following the end of the First World War, the outlook for architecture had been very bleak. Europe was debilitated and virtually at a standstill, and financial constraints meant that little construction work could be carried out even if there had been an abundance of labour and materials, which of course there was not. Hence the period was more one of intellectual activity than of building, and architects used this time to promote their new ideas.

Revolutionary idealism persisted throughout the decade, fading only in its last years as the result of the growth of a common disillusionment with those governments whose political programmes allowed no place for inventive architecture. Soviet constructivism was an art movement of determined abstraction, inspired by cubism and futurism but short-lived. It had its origins in the immediate pre-1917 October Revolution period, and the designs that emerged between then and 1923 broke completely from precedent in their ideas, social concepts and appearance.

The constructivist movement was symbolized by Vladimir Tatlin's interplay of spirals, a design project for the *Monument to the Third International* (1919–20). The key architectural ideas, or 'social condensers' of the constructivists were based on abstract post-revolutionary ideals. However these departures from convention were too radical for ready acceptance by the masses and the government alike, and the movement withered.

As in Soviet Russia, a similar revolutionary emotion was swelling among the more active groups of designers and artists in Germany, who were frustrated by the chaos they saw all around them. Among architects there was an inclination towards social buildings, but in Germany and in Europe generally there were insufficient resources for expensive building programmes, and the workers' clubs and cultural centres had to remain imaginary.

In expressionism, which could be said to have started to gather momentum in German architecture from about 1910, the desire for an exploration of new shapes and new solutions went hand in glove with investigations into new materials and techniques of construction. This combination led to a number of fascinating and highly idiosyncratic but impractical solutions such as those found in the drawings of Hermann Finsterlin, but although hardly anything was built, this expressionist interlude was one of the main catalysts for the development of modernism in architecture.

The Weimar Bauhaus was founded and staffed by mostly expressionist artists and designers who were trying to find more practical solutions. Under the directorship of Walter Gropius they sought a more integrated approach and, following exposure to Theo van Doesburg's *de Stijl* around 1923, the rectilinear modern style became an integral part of the Bauhaus philosophy.

Such architects in Germany as Erich Mendelsohn, Peter Behrens and Hans Scharoun evolved a functional and practical form of expressionism which related logical planning and the formal ideas for a new architecture to external and artistic goals. This was largely based on the nineteenth-century idea that 'form follows function', and was to become known as functionalism. Simply put, if a building and its machine elements function efficiently, then by definition its form will be aesthetically appropriate and pleasing architecture.

Below: *symbolic of the whole constructivist movement was* Vladimir Tatlin's unbuilt project *for a* Monument to the Third International, *1919–20, which, through its interplay of spirals, evoked a new kind of architectural monumentalism*

Expressionism

The expressionist architects, like the painters of *die Brücke* and *der Blaue Reiter* groups centred on Germany between 1910–1925, sought peculiarly personal, even bizarre, visual forms and effects. Among the earliest expressionistic buildings were the highly individual early works of Hans Poelzig, such as the Luban chemical factory, Germany, 1911–12 (*right*), and the municipal water tower, Posen, Germany (now Poznan, Poland), 1911.

The second generation of expressionists was active after the First World War in both Germany and the Netherlands, and was responsible for dynamically sculpted structures such as the Einstein Observatory, Potsdam, 1920, by Erich Mendelsohn.

Functionalism

Zweckkunst, functional art, is most closely described in architectural theory according to three ideas:
• no building is beautiful unless it properly fulfills its function;
• if a building fulfills its function it is therefore beautiful;
• since form relates to function, all artifacts, including buildings, are a kind of industrial or applied art.

The third of these propositions is generally credited to the architect Gottfried Semper, who originated the theory in a nineteenth-century book on arts and crafts. Of the three key propositions, this has had the most influence, since it is closely akin to a theory of aesthetics in that it regards all visual arts as generically related.

Weimar Bauhaus

Although Walter Gropius had founded the school by combining the Weimar Academy of Arts with the School of Applied Arts in 1919, the architecture department (*Hochschule für Gestaltung*, literally 'academy for form giving') was not established until 1927. The Bauhaus ('house of building') was at Weimar until 1925, when it moved to Dessau (*below*) on the promise of better financial support and to escape the increasing antagonism of the conservative Weimar community. There it remained until 1932, when it was transferred to Berlin before being forced to close by the Nazi régime in 1933.

Although Gropius had designed the administration, educational and residential quarters at Dessau, and so Bauhaus members had had an effective immersion in architecture from the beginning, the richly diverse remit of the Bauhaus workshops officially did not include the teaching of architecture until the appointment as chairman of

the Swiss architect Hannes Meyer, in 1927. Even so, because its didactic method was based on the assumption that, if one could design anything, one could design everything (in the words of its founder 'The approach to any kind of design – a chair, a building, a whole town or a regional plan – should be essentially identical') then probably architecture was always on the agenda.

Gropius resigned in 1928, whereupon Meyer became director, a position he held until 1930, when it was suggested that he should resign because of his left-wing political views that had brought

him into conflict with the Dessau authorities. Ludwig Mies van der Rohe was the director from then until its forced closure in 1933.

The Bauhaus commanded a far-reaching respect and influence, its workshop products being widely copied and reproduced. Even today, our widespread acceptance of functional, unornamented designs for objects of daily use owes much to the Bauhaus precept and example.

Right: *night-time at the Schocken Department Store, Stuttgart, Germany, 1926–28, by Erich Mendelsohn, showing one of the two fully-glazed main stair towers in the centre*

De Stijl

This Dutch movement, influenced by cubism, first came to the fore in Leiden in 1917 and remained active until being dissolved in 1931. It included among its members the painters Piet Mondrian and Theo van Doesburg, and the architects Jacobus Johannes Pieter Oud and Gerrit Thomas Rietveld. They advocated a severe and precise economy of line and form, austerely pristine surfaces, and purity of colour.

As a group, *de Stijl* influenced not only architecture but also painting and the decorative arts, including furniture design, but the movement realised its stylistic aims mainly through architecture. The Workers' Housing Estate in Hoek van Holland, 1924–27, *below*, designed by Oud, expresses the same clarity and order of line so noticable in Mondrian's paintings; as does Rietveld's Schroeder House, Utrecht, 1924, with the severe purity of its façade. The Schroeder House is Rietveld's masterpiece and is remarkable for its interplay of right-angled forms, planes and lines and for its use of primary colours.

Theo van Doesburg was the pseudonym of Christian Emil Marie Küpper (1883–1931), a founding member and leader of the group. He also founded the *avant-garde* art review *De Stijl*, a publication that continued until his death.

He wrote his manifesto, *De Stijl*, in 1926, explaining his aesthetic concept based on the use of inclined planes in geometric abstract paintings to increase the dynamic effect of the composition.

Above: *Café De Unie, Rotterdam, 1925, by Jacobus Johannes Pieter Oud*

One rather simplistic approach to resolving architectural problems within this aesthetic framework is now known as pragmatic functionalism. This followed the line that it was possible to design a common shell, which by the manipulation of the internal organisation of the building could be used for a different purpose on a variety of sites, and this flexibility itself was the logical expression of the building's function.

A third element that also existed was the one popularised by Henry-Russell Hitchcock and Philip Johnson, known as international functionalism. This was exemplified by the German Werkbund in its 1927 Stuttgart Exhibition and in the writings of Le Corbusier, and is best identified as a clear, white, rectangular, concrete architecture, stark and unembellished.

Also in 1927, Hannes Meyer and Le Corbusier submitted competition designs for the League of Nations Headquarters, Geneva, Switzerland, which were among the first attempts to create

Walter Gropius

He regarded architecture and design as an ever-changing spectrum, always related to the contemporary world. He championed the belief that it was the architect's duty to encompass the total visual environment, and he himself designed furniture, an automobile and a railcar. He emphasised housing and city planning, the usefulness of sociology, and the necessity of using specialist teams for each specific task.

Gropius designed the school building and faculty housing when the Bauhaus moved to Dessau. The school itself is a key monument of modern architecture and Gropius' best-known building. This dynamic composition of asymmetrical plan has smooth white walls set with horizontal windows, and a flat roof.

Right: *Weißenhof Estate, 21 buildings at the heart of the Werkbund Exhibition, Stuttgart, Germany, 1927. This mix of single-family dwellings and apartments was the work of 17 architects*

Deutscher Werkbund

This labour league was founded in 1907 in München by artists, artisans and architects who designed mass-produced industrial, commercial and household products and furnishings, as well as architecture.

Its intellectual leaders, the architects Hermann Muthesius and Henry van der Velde, were influenced by the English Arts and Crafts movement. Their aim as a collaborative enterprise was to revive industrial crafts applied to machine-made goods, and they were determined that form should be dictated only by function and that unnecessary ornamentation should be eliminated.

Muthesius' ideas were adopted by the Werkbund in 1914, advocating the maximum use of mechanical mass production and standardized design, and rejecting the individual artistic expression championed by another Werkbund faction led by van der Velde.

Similar organisations were founded in Austria (1912) and Switzerland (1913) and England's Design and Industries Association adopted similar aims, in 1915.

The Deutscher Werkbund exhibited notable examples of architecture in steel, concrete and glass in Köln in 1914. These included a theatre by van der Velde, an administrative office building, the Pavilion for the Deutz machinery factory and garages designed by Walter Gropius.

Following the First World War, the Werkbund re-established itself with an exhibition in Stuttgart in 1927, organised by Ludwig Mies van der Rohe, displaying his own work with that of Gropius and Le Corbusier, all of which had a high degree of standardization of materials and design. It also took part in the Paris exhibition of industrial arts and building which was organised by Gropius, László Moholy-Nagy, Marcel Breuer and Herbert Bayer in 1930, although it disbanded in 1933 as the Nazis took power in Germany.

Above: *the first tubular steel chair, 1925, by Marcel Breuer, went unnoticed until the Werkbund's sensational 1927 exhibition*

Right: *4, rue Mallet-Stevens, Passy, Paris, 1927, by Mallet-Stevens (1886–1945), and,* far right, *number 6. The architect was the co-founder of the* Union des Artistes Modernes, *along with Pierre Chareau, and this street of nominally modernist houses is the first example anywhere of early Art Deco*

a prestigious modern building complex within the new idiom; however, the projects were never built. Still in 1927, but this time in New York, a Machine Age Exposition was held. The modern style had not been widely known in America during the 1920s, and the exposition was billed as the first 'major event in the modern movement in America'. An unjust claim, given that the event displayed simple machine parts and products side by side with Russian constructivist art and photographs of contemporary European buildings, and chose to ignore the fact that the 'new' architecture had already established firm roots on the west coast through the works of Richard Josef Neutra and Rudolph Michael Schindler, although their work was not of skyscraper proportions, being mainly on a domestic scale.

There was still no international understanding on exactly where the future of twentieth-century architecture lay; what is more, there was no official international body to debate it. The Exhibition of Decorative Arts that had been held in Paris in 1925 had displayed little affinity with the work of radical architects, but nevertheless

Art Deco

A movement in architecture and the decorative arts from 1925, which developed into a major style in western Europe and the United States during the 1930s. Art Deco design represented modernism translated into fashion; its products included both individually-crafted luxury items and mass-produced wares, but it fell from favour during the Second World War.

Its distinguishing features are simple, clean shapes, often with a 'streamlined' appearance; ornament that is geometric or stylised from representational forms; and usually varied, frequently expensive materials, which often include man-made substances such as bakelite, vita-glass and ferroconcrete, as well as natural ones including jade, ivory, silver, obsidian, chrome and rock-crystal.

Most of the outstanding Art Deco creators designed individually-crafted or limited-edition items. They include furniture designers; metalsmiths; glass, jewellery and fashion designers; artist jewellers and figurative sculptors in addition to the most notable architect in the style, Eliel Saarinen.

The most monumental embodiments of Art Deco are the Rockefeller Center (especially its interiors, supervised by Donald Deskey), the Chrysler Building, by William Van Alen, and the Empire State Building, by Shreve, Lamb & Harmon, all in New York.

Donald Deskey 1894–1989

An American designer, who was educated at the University of California, Berkeley, the Mark Hopkins Institute for Art (now the San Francisco Art Institute), the Art Institute of Chicago, completed his studies in Paris, 1920–22, and helped to establish industrial design as a profession.

He was director of the art department at Juniata College, Huntington, Pennsylvania, and later the director of the industrial design department of New York University, where his work received international recognition.

Advertising was his first employment, then furniture and interior design; his inventive use of industrial materials for decorative purposes brought him a contract in 1932 from the Rockefeller Center, Inc. for the interior decoration and furnishings for Radio City Music Hall. He went on to produce a number of projects for various world's fairs.

Left: *the main entrance to the Hoover Building, Perivale, Middlesex, 1932–36, by Wallis, Gilbert; Britain's most renowned example of the Art Deco style*

Below right: *Villa Savoye,
Poissy-sur-Seine, near Paris,
1928–1931, by Le Corbusier
and his cousin Pierre Jeanneret; a
series of ramps and staircases rises
from the entrance lobby to connect
the different levels. The terrace
garden is connected to the living
rooms by large strip windows and
sliding glass walls. This building
was to prove to be one of the
seminal works of twentieth-century
architecture*

reflected some interesting superficial resemblances to international functional architecture and some of the characteristics of these hard-core modernists. Initially the style was generally overlooked by architectural historians because it lacked a consistent aesthetic; but, in a direct contrast with functionalism, it did incorporate many applied decorative features including zigzag surface patterns, rounded arches, curved corner details, and elaborate 'ship-prow' embellishments, many carried out in synthetic materials with mirror surfaces or in a black finish. It gained popular international acclaim, and the style known today as Art Deco, *Moderne* or even Jazz Age Modern, is remembered for this characteristic decoration. For most of the serious architects of the day, the style was a showy, attention-seeking form of modernism, best reserved for decorating popular places of entertainment.

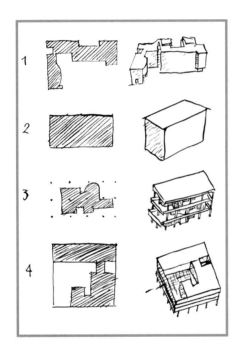

Above: *Le Corbusier's
les quatres compositions,
1929; 1 shows the La Roche and
Jeanneret duplex;
2, the pure cube of the Villa
Stein, Garches;
3, the Dom-ino system of the
gridded reinforced concrete
skeleton in which plans can
develop freely, and
4, the Villa Savoye, Poissy, is a
smooth prism raised on stilts*

Following a two-day meeting between 26–29 June 1928 of Le Corbusier and his fellow-Swiss, the art historian Siegfried Giedion, the *Congrès Internationaux d'Architecture Moderne* (CIAM) was formed. Gropius was also in attendance, and the central intention of those present was to return architecture to 'its true sphere, which is economic, sociological and altogether at the service of humanity'. This movement was to develop into a highly influential arena for the advancement of the modern machine-age style. The first major meeting of the new organisation took place the following year in Frankfurt-am-Main, under the direction of Ernest May, and its main topic of debate was low-cost housing.

It was the earnest desire of those architects associated with CIAM that the principles that they had established should gain international acceptance. Groups in Belgium, Britain, Greece, the Netherlands, Spain and Switzerland all contributed to CIAM congresses and working groups, with each group confronting and dealing with the problems that ranged in scale from the single house to city planning.

The final years of the decade were among the most productive for architects, brought to a dramatic end by the collapse of Wall Street in 1929 and the ensuing Depression. This had the effect of curtailing much projected building in America and elsewhere, particularly in Germany and the Soviet Union, where the political atmosphere was rapidly hardening on anti-cultural lines. By this time modern architecture was established and the former radicals had become successful contemporary practitioners.

The 1930s

Although the Second World War did not begin until 1939, German architects, especially Jews, had been leaving Germany even before the rise of Nazism in 1933 and that country ceased to be the centre of inspiration of the modern style. Internationalism became a reality within the first few years of the 1930s as the artists, designers and architects who had been forced into exile began practising the tenets of the modern movement in their adopted homelands. Many stayed at least temporarily in the UK.

Le Corbusier, however, remained and he became the most powerful figure in European architecture, with CIAM retaining its position as a unifying force and influence for the modern movement. Both Gropius and Mies van der Rohe had decamped to America and to new opportunities. During the 1930s modern architecture gained a firm foothold throughout the world as the élite architects, scattered by the conditions of impending war, were paradoxically united in their efforts, to the extent that by the middle of the decade many countries had at least one or two buildings which clearly resulted from the influence of Le Corbusier, CIAM or its dispersed members.

Left: *Casa del Fascio, Como, Italy, 1932–36, by Giuseppe Terragni, a white marble-clad building that was square in plan around an internal courtyard*

Modernism

Modernism emerged in Europe prior to the First World War, and reached its peak in the architecture of the 1920s and 1930s. Its aesthetic derived from functionalism, that had embraced new technology, rejected ornament and aspired to create new solutions for architecture and urban design that were appropriate to the prevailing conditions of the twentieth century. Functionalist thinking, however, led to an increased use of the materials that the machine is capable of producing, such as plastics, synthetic fibres, and acrylic paints.

Modernist buildings characteristically had asymmetrical compositions, unrelieved cubic shapes, an absence of mouldings, white rendering, open plans and metal and glass construction that gave rise to large windows in horizontal bands.

The International style

When the modernist manner reached the USA with Neutra and Schindler, it was reborn as the international style. Its boxlike forms, its hard glassy surfaces, its use of metal tubing and plywood, and its lack of colour and of ornament were felt by many to reflect a lack of human warmth. Le Corbusier's famous dictum that the house is a machine had brought the retort that most people do not like living in machines.

Later emigrants to the USA such as Bauhaus architect Mies van der Rohe, and others, led to a second flowering there of the international style, in 1945–60, but by the 1970s it had declined into corporate modernism, and postmodernism followed in the 1980s.

This initial international crop of derivative modern buildings was constructed in concrete with all of the hallmarks of the new style, with flat roofs, plain, white surfaces, long narrow horizontal windows, versatile interiors and cubic exteriors.

There was a brief time while the critics appeared to hold off, before these new buildings began to appear on the pages of the architectural journals, but soon each new construction was eagerly reported and the white aesthetic images began to fill the glossy pages. The pictures portrayed perhaps did give the impression of an over-simplification of the new architecture, but they helped to spread the word and create a demand. Soon picture books on modern houses, apartment blocks, industrial and institutional buildings proliferated, just like the buildings, on a worldwide scale. Perhaps most pleasingly, they even appeared in those European countries from which their original proponents had come. With hindsight we can see that modern architecture had arrived and the success of its leaders was assured.

This welcome was far from being immediate or universal, however. Some local authorities in England discriminated and were obstructive by refusing building permissions; in the Soviet Union there was a more systematic suppression of the modern movement's ideas, while in Germany every attempt was made to replace the radical work of the past few years with a monumental nationalistic architecture that would now be considered ugly.

Following the Machine Age Exposition of 1927 in New York there was an exhibition devoted to the international style in 1931, at the Museum of Modern Art in New York. It was concerned with international architecture since 1922, and included work from fifteen countries.

Henry-Russell Hitchcock and Philip Johnson re-used the term *International Style* for a book written at the same time as the New York exhibition, though not published until the following year. A feature of both the book and the exhibition was the emphasis on the number of architects who had been producing work with many common aims and characteristics. These architects can be termed the second-generation pioneers, and include Le Corbusier, Mies van der Rohe, Walter Gropius and Johannes Oud, all of whom were intent on the development of a style with a universal validity.

From then until the end of the decade, as this second generation of architects and their contemporaries began to interpret the work of the pioneers, they began to realise the limitations of the fundamental characteristics of universality and uniformity of the new international architecture, which disregarded such basic restrictions as weather, as well as traditional national solutions and preferences. The plain white walls of concrete, though harmonious with the Mediterranean, did not transfer well to other countries; flat roofs, though perfect under the sun, were clearly

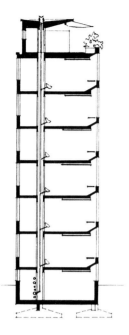

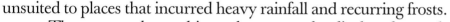

Far left: *a section through the patients' accommodation of the Tuberculosis Sanatorium, Paimio, Finland, 1929–33, by Alvar Aalto, a tall slim block which was designed to provide the maximum exposure to sun and air;* left, *the exterior of the Sanatorium, which was financially a co-operative undertaking by over fifty communities; and* above, *a view along one of the corridors leading to a communal room*

Below: *the main gallery of the public library, Viipuri, Finland, 1930–35, by Alvar Aalto*

unsuited to places that incurred heavy rainfall and recurring frosts.

There were other architects, however, who displayed a much more practical attitude to the new architecture, seen in the work of the Finnish Alvar Aalto. This clearly indicated an architect who could embrace the new style while not abandoning the traditional aspects of Finnish architecture. Aalto's buildings made a very positive contribution to their environment in both scale and relationship to the landscape; his two major works, both of which were important buildings of the modern movement, were the Viipuri Library, 1930–35, and the Paimio Sanatorium, 1929–33.

Convincing a dubious client or a sceptical public of the merits of a new approach has always been an inevitable obstacle for radical architects, and on the whole it was left to the more wealthy and enlightened clients to commission innovative work. In the Netherlands, however, Johannes Oud was the City Architect

Left: *a perspective drawing of an aerial view of the Blijdorp Estate, Rotterdam, 1931, by J J P Oud*

of Rotterdam and thus was able to exert an effective influence not only on his own municipality, but also to some extent upon others in the Netherlands. It is possible to suggest that because of the exceptional talents of Aalto, the distribution of population and the availability of sites in Finland, he was able to exert a single powerful influence there. In Germany there had been little development since the previous decade, but the status quo was abruptly overturned when the National Socialists gained political control. First Paul Ludwig Troost was chosen to express the party's aspirations towards a monumental community architecture, then after his death, Albert Speer became the stage designer for Nazi pageantry.

Throughout Europe in the 1930s the new international style of architecture was seen mainly in villa designs, expensive apartments, retail outlets and other commercial and industrial buildings. In Britain as elsewhere, the Second World War put a temporary stop to the promise and progress of modern architecture in its first decade of development.

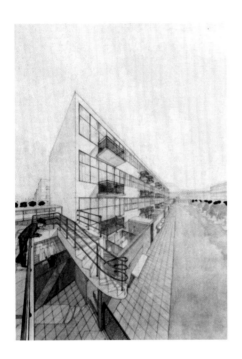

Above and below: *two views of Blijdorp, from balcony level*

The 1940s

Architecture in Europe generally was virtually at a standstill between 1939 and 1945; money was scarce and commissions were harder to find than ever, and anything that was available was invariably concerned with the war effort. In Scandinavia, however, there was a minor reaction to functional architecture in that there was a return to more traditional forms and materials. This was also the case in Switzerland, a neutral country during the war, which concentrated on housing and planning issues.

Those European architects who had left their homelands in order to escape the war in many instances had passed through

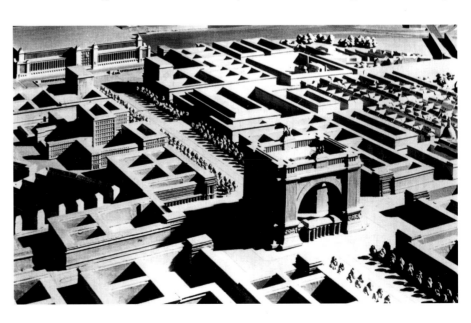

Right: *Albert Speer's 1937 plan for a new Berlin, that was intended to have been built after the Nazis' victory at the end of the Second World War*

Britain on their way west. Many joined the Modern Architectural Research Group (MARS) in the late 1930s, enabling this London-based practice to become a powerful national force for the new architecture. On reaching their new utopia, these architects were soon engaged on a number of large-scale projects in both north and south America, disseminating the ideas of modern architecture.

The war created many new opportunities for industry in the USA, providing a much-needed impetus after the Wall Street crash of 1929. These in turn demanded new buildings, such as aircraft factories, and the architects and engineers who provided these solutions had visions of a technologically-based building industry. Richard Buckminster Fuller was one such visionary.

The immensity of the reconstruction necessary after the war in Europe was awesome. Complete towns and cities had to be rebuilt, and everyone had an interest in their successful design. Initially, in the UK quick fixes had to be found and implemented to erect new homes for the demobbed military and the refugees alike; many of these were intended to be temporary, pre-fabricated homes. The Temporary Housing Programme of 1944–48 was supposed to provide half a million bungalows, of which perhaps a third were built, of concrete, asbestos or aluminium sheeting on the outside. These were designed in great detail as complete self-contained units with fitted kitchens and bathrooms, which could be very quickly put up, and were so successful and popular that some were still in use thirty years later.

Carefully-considered, longer-term planning was possible for individual suburbs and communities in France, and for the towns in the land-hungry Netherlands. In Germany, which had an altogether more extensive program to contemplate, morale was low among the architects and artists who had remained in the country throughout the war years and it took many years for the few practices that were formed to become effective.

The architects who had built according to CIAM and Corbusian principles in the 1930s were now widely dispersed or in most cases had closed their practices, and so after the war a so-called 'modern functional style' became the accepted mode in which to work almost anywhere. Eventually the technical excellence, functional organisation and aesthetic idealism that had been implicit in the new architecture from the beginning became visible and very widespread. Along with these came a new expressive freedom that was derived from the projects of leaders such as Frank Lloyd Wright and Le Corbusier, whose disciples now began to push at the boundaries of twentieth-century architecture.

Le Corbusier himself had been absent from Paris between 1940 and 1944, returning to France to pursue his new human-scale monumentality. This was the expression of his proportional system based on the human body, which he applied to all his designs, and and resulted in his vast *Unité d'habitation*, Marseilles,

Above: *the Wichita House, 1944–46, by Richard Buckminster Fuller, was a modified version of his Dymaxion House of 1927, and was produced by the Beech Aircraft Corporation as an experiment, using industrially-manufactured aircraft components*

Below: *Le Corbusier's Marseilles apartment block,* Unité d'habitation, *1946–52. This gigantic concrete slab of a city was 137 m (450 ft) long, 20 m (66 ft) deep and about 61 m (200 ft) tall*

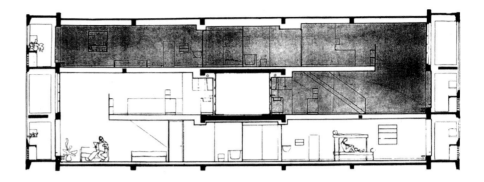

Right (elevation): Unité d'habitation, *Marseilles, contains almost 340 apartments of varying sizes for some 1,600 people. It is comprised of 15 apartment floors plus a two-storey shopping street which runs the length of the building, about one-third of the way up. Two rows* of pilotis *(foundation piles) hold up the building, on top of which is a communal roof garden,* below

Right: *Le Corbusier's plan for the reconstruction of the centre of Saint Dié, 1945. He proposed to locate the manufacturing plants to the south, by the river Meurthe. Ramps and bridges from all directions gave access to both the large apartment blocks to the east of the central area, and the pedestrian plaza on the north bank*

France, which occupied him from the end of the war until 1952. He had thought that he would finally be able to apply his theories of planning in the reconstruction of France, and in 1945 prepared plans for the cities of Saint-Dié and La Pallice-Rochelle. At Saint-Dié, in the Vosges mountains, he proposed rehousing the 30,000 inhabitants of the destroyed town into five functional skyscrapers.

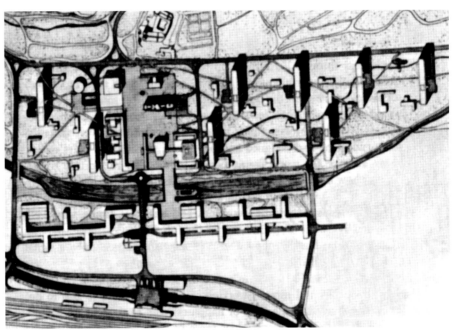

These plans were rejected, but they subsequently circulated throughout the world and their principles became widely accepted. Le Corbusier's embitterment was only compounded when he was named as a member of the jury of architects for the construction of the United Nations building, New York, instead of being asked to design it himself.

In Britain, the Group Planning Committee of MARS published its scheme for the renewal and reconstruction of London in 1942. It had been drawn up originally in 1938, but gained new impetus and relevance on publication, following the extensive war damage to central London. The plan, which adopted the CIAM approach of a hierarchical structure for a city, took in the whole of the greater London area and linked the various zones for housing, industry and recreation by a series of service and distributor roads to a central, linear, east-west autoroute.

It was interpreted too literally by those responsible for the building of British new towns, however, and so the MARS plan was effectively ignored, as 'precinct' planning became the flavour of the day. Unfortunately the precinct concept overlooked the development of personal transport, which subsequently has continued to increase exponentially.

Across the Atlantic, the USA was already attuned to the growing popularity of the car after the war. There had been already a spreading web of turnpike roads, precursors of the freeways, across the continent by 1940. These encouraged people to use their cars for leisure enjoyment, and a new linear urban pattern began to emerge, with motels, drive-in movies, diners, stores and restaurants all being redesigned to cater for in-car living.

Along with this new outlook and revitalisation that the the

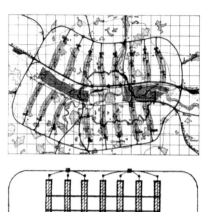

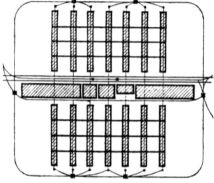

Top: *the MARS Group Planning Committee's* Plan for London, *1938–42, showing the general structure in relation to a map of London, and,* above, *as a schematic drawing*

Left: *860–880 North Lake Shore Drive apartments, Chicago, Illinois, 1948–51, by Mies van der Rohe*

freedom of the car epitomised, there were other economic factors that resulted in another significant change in urban America in the late 1940s. For while much of Europe was accommodated in temporary housing, the USA was enjoying postwar prosperity and the beginning of a new skyscraper age. Great apartment and office blocks with walls of lightweight glass and metal were being erected, the benchmark being set by architects such as Mies van der Rohe's Lake Shore Drive Apartments, Chicago, and Pietro Belluschi's Equitable Savings Building, Portland, Oregon 1944–47.

The 1950s

As architects and planners returned to work and training after the war, they resumed very much where they had left off, continuing with ideas for an architecture that had its roots firmly established in the prewar period. There was a very general acceptance of CIAM tenets and the so-called international functionalist style. In parallel with this there was also still an architecture which encompassed the more decorative interior, furniture and domestic design that owed much to the continuance of Art Deco and *moderne* ideas, mainly derived from prewar exhibitions.

The 'new architecture' of the 1950s was now in the hands of a third generation of designers who were generally considered less competent, less original and less experimental than their predecessors of the Bauhaus and the followers of Le Corbusier. The work of the second generation, particularly that of Le Corbusier, Mies van der Rohe and Alvar Aalto, was being exploited and copied on a far greater scale than before.

Building restrictions after the war were not lifted in Great

Above: *the Finnish Pavilion, World Fair, New York, 1939, by Alvar Aalto; its sweeping walls, three storeys high, defined the internal space. The walls leaned forward slightly, deviating from the vertical, each storey also being set forward, thus emphasising the sense of continuous movement*

Right: *this section of the interior of the Pavilion shows the various wood constructions used (wooden supports, tree sections)*

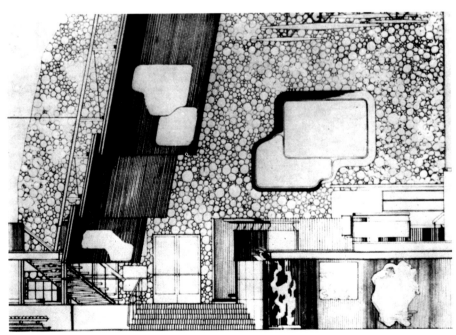

Britain until 1954, and there was little private building prior to that date. More than 30 pavilions erected on London's South Bank formed the venue for the Festival of Britain in 1951. In addition to commemorating the Great Exhibition of 1851, its purpose was to show the way forward for housing, and incidentally to provide a little colourful relief from years of austerity.

The central building was the Dome of Discovery by Ralph Tubbs, then the largest aluminium domed structure in the world, while the cigar-shaped Skylon by Powell and Moya was used to symbolize the whole exhibition. A model estate at Lansbury, north Poplar, and its associated school building schemes that had been laid out from 1946, was used as a live architecture exhibit to demonstrate the possibilities for an optimum living environment.

The reconstruction and rejuvenation of the great cities of mainland Europe such as Prague and Warsaw was underway, as was the rebuilding and repair of the medieval towns of Germany and France. There was a strong argument in favour of pulling down these ancient buildings and replacing them with completely modern cities, but conservation won the day. In view of the great necessity also to rebuild morale, it must be considered that this was the most humane and sensitive course of action to follow.

Thus practising architects throughout Europe went back to the history books, gained a deeper knowledge and understanding of the buildings that seemingly always had been there, and then repaired them by the application of modern materials and constructional methods to recapture their beauty.

Architects of this new generation, however competent at repairing the older buildings, were not experienced at town planning and tended to accede to the whims of municipal bodies, New Town Commissioners, commercial firms and other private

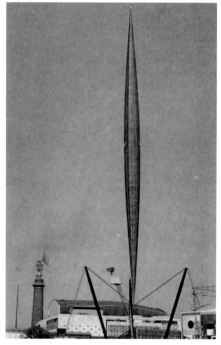

Above: *the 76.2 m (250 ft) high Skylon, Festival of Britain, London, 1951, by Sir Philip Powell of Powell and Moya; this elegant metal pencil was covered in aluminium louvres and lit from inside*

Left: *the UNESCO Headquarters building, Paris, 1953–58, under the control of Marcel Breuer and Pier Luigi Nervi, was one of the most important and architecturally distinguished buildings of the period; Y-shaped and eight storeys high, it had a reinforced-concrete free-standing entrance canopy*

clients. In this way, decisions on architectural matters were often made by those who did not fully understand their constraints. This resulted in a mismatch between the situation of housing where there were no communal facilities, and conversely shops or civic and leisure amenities that were not easily accessible, and so it was difficult for a community spirit to thrive. These ill-considered initiatives combined with a conservative aesthetic resulted in a quasi-modernistic architecture of dull design without any benefits in comfort or convenience. This pathetic approach has left us with a heritage since the Act of 1946 of eight New Towns in the London region and six in other parts of the UK, which along with the rebuilt central areas of cities such as Plymouth, are woefully disappointing. Furthermore, hindsight has now identified errors such as these as a possible cause of social problems.

There was also a lack of impetus at CIAM, where the elder generation of architects, who had long made their reputations, still held sway but had individually developed their ideas to the point of idiosyncracy. Then, in 1956, a group of young radicals under the name of Group X (ten) brought matters to a head. Although CIAM tottered on for further three years, the younger architects felt very strongly that the older-established members of the congress were applying abstract ideals and concepts impersonally to the practical problems of urban living. Of course, this is after all a normal reaction of ideas, one generation expressing its feelings about the preceding generation's outdatedness, and the resulting desire to create a new order. In this respect architecture is no different from pop music, transportation or any other social phenomenon.

The first coherent sign of this reaction was the New Brutalism, a term that had been coined as early as 1954 by the British architect, Alison Smithson, who later became a member of Group X. It has since come to be used as a description applied to a variety of architectural designs, many of which can be said to be based on an attitude of execution rather than actual structure. It is probably now best defined as a combination of the clarity of form that can be found in Le Corbusier's postwar projects and the logic of the structures of van der Rohe; essentially an honest approach to design and execution of the work.

Below: *a general view of Hunstanton Secondary Modern School, 1949–54, by Alison and Peter Smithson, which formulated the style known as New Brutalism. This was inspired by Le Corbusier's* Unité d'habitation, *Marseilles, and relied heavily on rough exposed concrete surfaces but the detailing relies more on the work of Mies van der Rohe;* above, *the gymnasium*

Significant advances were being made by the late 1950s in England, in both the industrialisation and re-fabrication of the public sector. The school building programme and public-authority housing were going ahead particularly briskly, and at the same time in the USA a new kind of formalism was emerging while Japan was awakening to functionalism. Meanwhile, Le Corbusier had already given the entire world a jolt with the unveiling of his remarkable Chapel at Ronchamp. His 'sacred task' changed the public perception of modern architecture for ever.

Before the decade of the 1950s came to an end, Frank Lloyd Wright made another highly individual statement. His Guggenheim Museum, New York, which was completed in 1959, just a few months after the architect's death, was as mould-breaking in its way as Le Corbusier's masterpiece.

Above: *the Crown Hall, Illinois Institute of Technology, 1956, by Mies van der Rohe; a large single-space building measuring 67 m (220 ft) by 36.5 m (120 ft) by 6 m (20 ft) high, the superstructure for which was built from four giant steel girders that were delivered to the site prefabricated*

Left: *the Chapel of Notre Dame-du-haut, Ronchamp, France, 1955, by Le Corbusier, showing its great shell-like roof and tiny windows*
Right: *Wright's popular Solomon R Guggenheim Museum, a wonderful spiral gallery topped by a glass dome*

The 1960s

Above: *Ron Herron's* Walking City *illustration, a huge structure that moved around on giant legs, as its inhabitants pleased, and below, his Archigram colleague Peter Cook's illustration for a* Plug-in City, *where dwellers in a future metropolis could unplug their entire living unit and move on; no more packing!*

Below: *Peace Pavilion, Hiroshima, Japan, 1956, by Kenzo Tange; a cultural hall reconciling the forms of traditional Japanese temples with modern concrete architecture, in what had been the city centre before Hiroshima's destruction in April 1945, by US B-29 bombers*

This decade was a transitional period, with the passing of the old masters; Frank Lloyd Wright had already died in 1959, and was to be followed by Le Corbusier in 1965, Mies van der Rohe and Walter Gropius in 1969 and Richard Neutra in 1970. A new generation of modern designers, such as Eero Saarinen and Pier Luigi Nervi, were beginning to make their mark.

With the death of Wright as well as the demise of CIAM, there was no longer any organisational institution to oversee and care for the health of modern architecture. Experimental freedom became available to any architect; the opportunity was gratefully seized, and and it became a time for fantasising.

This apparent urgency to reject whatever had existed before promoted an abundance of imaginative ideas, though many were completely unrelated to costs and thus were untenable. Look at Ron Herron's notional *Walking City*, 1964, or Peter Cook's *Plug-in City*, 1966, to glean some understanding of the direction in which design thinking was moving. Both of these appear to be offering an engineering solution to architectural problems.

The next generation of graduating architects was able to take advantage of cheaper, quicker air travel throughout the world and began to establish a forum for the exchange of ideas. This informal, loose-knit arrangement was promoted primarily by personal contact and grew into a world-wide network by the end of the decade. It was supported by the publication of numerous magazines and journals, road shows and exhibitions, and not least by the Buckminster Fuller World Design Decade programme.

As always, the discussion of particular points of view allowed by free exchange made new ideas more acceptable more quickly, even if only in theoretical terms. A groundswell of revolutionary thinking formed architectural opinion and attitudes, even if practical solutions to the building problems that these new ideas raised were less frequently presented. Modern architecture had the potential to became truly international in the 1960s; European and American architects worked in the middle and far east, while Japanese and Indian architects, many of whom had received their training in the West, took up positions and commissions in Europe and America. When engineers became partners in individual firms, their technical knowledge turned these ideas into realities.

This opening-up of the international design market had already begun with the work of such architects as Le Corbusier in the creation of the new capital of the Punjab at Chandigarh, 1951–56, and was continued into the 1960s by designers such as Louis Kahn with his work at Dhaka in Bangladesh, 1962, and the great Japanese architect Kenzo Tange, who epitomised this new internationalism.

Following exciting new skyscrapers such as the Seagram Building, Park Avenue, New York, 1958, by Mies van der Rohe with Philip Johnson and the older Lever Building, also in Park Avenue, 1952, by Skidmore, Owings & Merrill (SOM), the 1960s ushered in a more decorative use of exposed structural elements.

Below, left: the Inland Steel Building, 30 West Monroe Street, Chicago, 1957, by Skidmore, Owings & Merrill (SOM) was the first tall building to go up inside the Chicago Loop since the Depression. The supporting columns are inside the curtain wall, giving a forceful vertical emphasis to the construction, and can be compared with the building, below centre, that the firm was also involved in eight years

The use of metal as a revealed structural element, combined with new materials such as plastics and glass, became a characteristic of the 1960s. From the earlier use of cast and wrought iron in the previous century to the use of steel in frame constructions at the beginning of the twentieth century, industrial buildings and even some more public buildings had allowed their construction to show in the final form. During the 1960s the structural use of steel increasingly became thought of as a decorative element, thus linking structural requirement with design solutions.

The period also witnessed huge increases in the areas of air transportation, trade exhibitions and spectator sports, all of which made awesome demands upon the spatial resources of modern technology. Dulles International Airport, Chantilly, Virginia, was built to the design of Saarinen between 1958 and 1962. Rome's Pallazzo dello Sport was effected by Nervi in 1960; the stadia for the 1964 Olympic Games in Tokyo by Kenzo Tange; at the end of

later in the same city, the Richard J Daley Center, bounded by Washington, Randolph, Dearborn and Clark Streets, by C F Murphy Associates with SOM, and Loebl, Schlossman & Bennett. Its 31 storeys are comprised of three structural bays each 26.5 m (87 ft) long by about 14.6 m (48 ft) wide, with the long spandrels stretched across the façade-like bridge girders.
Above right: Richard Seifert's response to Chicago; Centre Point, London, 1966, a 34-storey Pop-Art era office block

Below: *the Post Office Tower,*
London, 1964, by Eric Bedford,
a thin concrete communications tower
of over 180 m (600 ft), that rises
from an eight-storey base. It was

clad in steel and glass, with a
public viewing gallery, and had a
revolving restaurant at the top
(closed since an IRA bomb that
shattered the windows in 1971)

Above: *the passenger terminal,*
Dallas International Airport,
Chantilly, Virginia, 1962–63, by
Eero Saarinen, which was completed
after the architect's death

the decade, and even into 1971, the McCormick Place exhibition hall, Chicago, was built by C F Murphy and Associates. Each of these constructions represents a colossal space articulated in reinforced concrete, steel and glass.

The World's Fair in New York of 1964 and the Montréal *Expo '67* both offered excellent showcase opportunities for the display of distinguished examples of modern architectural structures that demonstrated innovations in building technology. The Spanish pavilion by Javier Carvajal, and the Japanese pavilion by Maekawa Kunio made the most impression in 1964, while in 1967, the German pavilion by Frei Otto and the US pavilion by Buckminster Fuller received the acclaim in Montréal. Also at Montréal was the startling Constructivist apartment house, Habitat '67, by the Israeli, Moshe Safdie, in association with the David, Barrott Boulva firm, where 158 precast-concrete apartment units were hoisted into place and post-tensioned to permit dramatic cantilevers and terraces. The resulting ziggurat maximised the provision of privacy, fresh air and sunlight to the living spaces.

Above: *Habitat '67 by Moshe Safdie, a building complex situated in the Cité du Havre; it comprised a twelve-storey building, around which were arranged a series of one-family* *houses with large open terraces designed to accommodate 700 people in 158 dwellings*

Below: *the United States Pavilion, Expo '67, Montréal, 1967, by Buckminster Fuller; this 61 m (200 ft) high geodesic dome with a welded-steel spaceframe, covered in a transparent plastic sheeting, dominated the exhibition. The dome was constructed of a double layer, with triangular external elements and hexagonal inner elements over a total surface area of 13,099 m² (141,000 sq ft). A section through the dome, which had a diameter of 76.2 m (250 ft)*

Above and right: *the West German Pavilion, Expo '67, Montréal by Frei Otto and Rolf Gutbrod, comprised a cablenet roof (pre-stressed cable network) that covered an area of 7,432 m² (80,000 sq ft). It was covered in polyester cloth over stressed vinyl chloride sheets. Eight masts, the tallest reaching 38 m (125 ft), were used to carry the main cables*

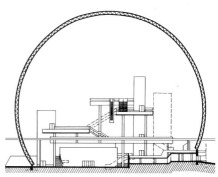

Above: *the Neue Nationalgalerie, Potsdamer Strasse 50, Berlin, 1967–68, by Ludwig Mies van der Rohe is a characteristic structure firmly rooted in the international style. The upper gallery is housed under a great coffered canopy which is supported by eight deeply-recessed cruciform steel columns and encased in walls of glass*

Left: *Tour Maine-Montparnasse, Paris, 1969–73, by Equipe AOM, was the first tall building to be built within the boundaries of the city of Paris. It was conceived as a multi-use complex and was sited above a métro station*

Reinforced concrete

Simplicity of manufacture, ease of application, flexibility in use, high tensile and compressive strength, are all properties that have made this the most universally applicable building material of the twentieth century. The development of prefabrication and interlocking units added to the simple rectilinear vocabulary of the modern aesthetic. On-the-spot shuttering soon became a widely practised and accepted effect, and because reinforced concrete has no predetermined form it was more frequently constructed in curved forms.

It was invented by Joseph Monnier as early as 1849, when it was called ferro-concrete, and in early use was important for its fire resistance, particularly for skyscraper construction. Thus it has been by far the most influential building material in terms of use and architectural form alike.

Right: *Sears Tower, 233 South Wacker Drive, Chicago, 1968–74, by Skidmore, Owings & Merrill, who used prefabricated steel units to speed up construction. Each unit consisted of a two-storey column 7.9 m (26 ft) high, with beams attached to each side, known by the ironworkers as a 'Christmas tree'. These trees were connected at the corner columns to create a tube 22.8 m (75 ft) square. The lower floors are a bundle of nine 22.8 m (75 ft) square tubes for a street-level footprint of 20.9 m² (225 sq ft), or one third of a city block. As these nine tubes rise, they stop at different heights. There are advantages to this construction; wind resistance is increased because of the bundling of the tubes, and bundling gives more lateral stiffness because each tube has its own structure. The bundled tube concept also uses less steel than conventional structures. The tower is 110 storeys, 443.12 m (1,454 ft) high*

The 1970s

Below: Centre National d'Art et de Culture Georges-Pompidou, *Paris, was conceived by the President in 1969, construction continuing from 1972, until its official inauguration on 31 January 1977. The design competition attracted 681 proposals, nearly 500 of them from outside France. The winning design was by Renzo Piano and Richard Rogers, in association with Gianfranco Franchini, John Young and Ove Arup & Partners.*

Some architects and critics had begun to baulk at the constraints and limitations inherent in the international style by this time. The stark and denuded qualities of the steel-and-glass boxes that embodied the style appeared stultifying and formulaic by then. The result was a reaction against these stereotypes and a renewed exploration of the possibilities of innovative design and decoration. Architects began creating freer, more imaginative structures that used modern building materials and decorative elements to create a variety of novel effects.

Robert Venturi had been one of the younger students of Louis Kahn, and he published his book *Complexity and Contradiction in Architecture* in 1966. Today Venturi's exposition is regarded as

Initially the Pompidou Centre was a shock for Parisians, with its multitude of external 'funnels' placed to ensure that inside nothing would hamper the use of space. As a result, the escalators are presented like architectural gangways and the services ducts look like curtains hanging at virtual windows on a stage. Close by, and at the same time, Parisians claimed back from the choking traffic the large wholesale market area of Les Halles, following a decision to remove the market trading to Rungis in 1962

Right: *Les Halles Forum, Paris, 1979, by Claude Vasconi and Georges Penchreac'h is an underground pedestrian complex on four levels, surrounding an open-air patio. The clear glass arcades provide natural light and open the complex to the surrounding district. Level Four provides the entrances to the Forum, together with shops and offices; Level Three is the main shopping and entertainment area, Level Two has a wide balcony set beneath windows and overlooking Place Basse, while Level One connects with the garden*

the foundation document of postmodernism, a movement that became prominent in the 1970s and early 1980s. Although it had a widespread international representation and so should be regarded as the successor to the international style, there were other reactions against this long-lived idiom.

There is such a diversity within the architecture that has been designated postmodern, however, that it is easier to recognise a building with postmodern elements than it is to describe the style. Generally speaking, in its most inclusive form, it has two basic characteristics. Most obviously, it is anti-modernist in its desire to avoid any association with the modern-style 'white box'. Further than this, it is inclusive rather than exclusive; the rational layouts and pure forms of the Bauhaus and its many followers have been superceded by a pluralism of style. Allusions or clear references to elements of classical architecture may be made, and colour and pattern may be used with a freedom that quite often produces startling effects.

Such characteristics are evident in vastly different guises in the AT&T Building (formerly the Chippendale Building), New York, by Philip Johnson, with its crowning classical pediment, and the Public Services Building, Portland, Oregon, USA, 1980–82, by Michael Graves, with its pedestal and use of colour.

The term postmodernism is now accepted as synonymous with anti-modernism. Europeans tend to regard postmodernism as being rooted in America, with the suspicion of being gratuitously disrespectful or disdainful of the whole western architectural tradition. The European style after modernism is more clearly influenced by the all-permeating consciousness of the classical tradition, and its development includes such large-scale works as those undertaken by the Catalan architect Ricardo Bofill both on the outskirts of Paris (*below:* Le Viaduc housing, St Quentin-en-Yvelines, 1974) and in Barcelona. Postmodernist features have since crept unconsciously into many major works although their designers were not formally identified as postmodernists.

Above: *the AT&T Building, New York, 1982, by Philip Johnson*
Below: *the Public Services Building, Portland, Oregon, 1980–82, by Michael Graves*

The 1980s

The period began as a time of economic excess, when a great deal of finance was being made available for architectural creativity. This momentum continued unabated until the stock market collapse of October 1987, after which most major projects that were already well advanced were completed, although some were cut back, but new ones were postponed or abandoned altogether. The collapse in land values and difficulty in letting commercial property, together with the uncertainty in Europe following the unification of Germany in 1989, forced many investors to put schemes on hold and the decade ended in an opposite mood.

In retrospect we can see that this provided the opportunity for architects and engineers to begin to appreciate the emerging advantages of cheap technology available in the studio. Computer-aided design is now an indespensible tool for both professions.

The Venice Biennale of 1980 included a series of postmodernist façades in the architectural section, *The Presence of the Past*, putting the style on a global level. Although postmodernism still could not be defined in terms of a specific set of stylistic and ideological characteristics, the exhibition did succeed in breaking down the barriers to understanding that existed between the contemporary and the traditional approaches to architecture. Postmodernist design did identify and establish links with traditional features from architectural history, but in its heyday relied essentially on the façade as a means of including them.

As a result, it is arguable that postmodernism reduced architecture to a package deal in which the developer determined the contents, and the architect the packaging or façade. Any city centre development has its high-rise towers, dressed in reflective glass envelopes or with devalued historical trappings of one kind or another. The leading architects of the previous decades, such as Mies van der Rohe and Louis Kahn, during the 1980s remained iconoclastically committed to a deconstruction of all historical

Below right: *one of the follies of Parc de la Villette, Paris, 1982–90, by Bernard Tschumi, together with,* below left, *a line drawing of the same folly, which was designed to function as a restaurant*

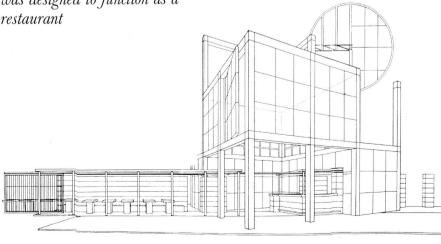

legacy and to a re-assembly of its precepts and components in accordance with the technological capacity of the epoch. The term *Neue Sachlichkeit* (New Objectivity) had been coined as long ago as the 1920s by van der Rohe to describe this analytical starting from first principles, concerning the intended function of the building.

A loose-knit group of five New York architects (Peter Eisenman, John Hejduk, Michael Graves, Charles Gwathmey and Richard Meier) had seen the *Neue Sachlichkeit* as an over-reductive approach, and in the 1960s committed themselves to the idea of an autonomous architecture. Its tenets were fully expressed by Bernard Tschumi, who won the competition in 1983 for the Parc de la Villette, Paris, a prototypical urban park for the twenty-first century. His playful design aspired to an anti-classical architecture in which unexpected configurations and uses would arise out of the red constructivist follies that punctuate the park. Tschumi differentiated between one folly and another by ringing the changes on a series of prisms, cylinders, stairs, ramps and canopies.

This led directly to an exhibition at the New York Museum of Modern Art (MoMA) in June 1988, for which the show catalogue was entitled *Deconstructivist Architecture*. The exhibition was based on the unbuilt work of Frank O Gehry, Daniel Libeskind, Rem Koolhaas (who had competed against Tschumi for the Parc de la Villette commission), Peter Eisenman, Zaha Hadid and Coop Himmelblau as well as Tschumi. Mark Wigley, the author of the exhibition catalogue, claimed that although deconstructivist architecture questions the implicit beliefs of architecture and the deeply-entrenched cultural assumptions about order, harmony, stability and unity which underlie these beliefs, this in itself is not new; what deconstructivism does is to expose the unfamiliar, hidden within the traditional. Logically it is therefore unsurprising that deconstructivism should not become a cohesive movement, but that the exhibitors at the MoMA show have remained amongst the most influential figures in international architecture; their originality of thought and personal inventiveness led to their continued success.

Gehry was unquestionably an outstanding pioneer of a movement that, at the end of the twentieth century, has helped to return architecture to its place as a major art. His Museum, Weil-am-Rhine, Germany, 1986–89, for the furniture manufacturer Vitra, is a marvellous statement of form that has integrated architecture with art in a sculptural structure that displays echoes of the unbuilt designs of the Russian constructivists and the German expressionists of the 1920s and 1930s.

Another of the MoMA 'magnificent seven' is Zaha Hadid, an architect acclaimed as an artist for her unbuilt work, whose style has best been described as 'exploded isometric projection'. Of her built work the Vitra Fire Station, 1993, on the same site as Gehry's Museum, is an arresting vision in concrete, steel and glass.

Above: *the* Neue Staatsgalerie, *Stuttgart, 1977–84, by* James Stirling, Michael Wilford *& Associates*
Below: *Vitra Museum, Weil-am-Rhine, Germany, 1986–89, by Frank O Gehry*

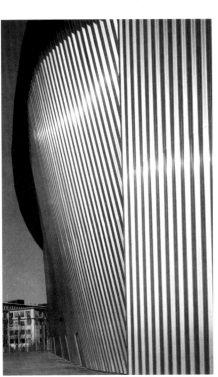

Hadid studied at the Architectural Association in London under Rem Koolhaas, whose own flamboyant approach to architecture can be found at its most impressive at the Euralille complex, Lille, France. Koolhaas and the Office of Metropolitan Architecture were awarded the commission in 1988, following the decision to use Lille as the TGV train terminal for the Channel Tunnel project, with Koolhaas as architect-in-chief. He was responsible for the design of the Grand Palais, a 50,000 m² (538,200 sq ft) convention centre that cost just FF350m because of the extensive use of a variety of inexpensive materials such as corrugated plastic for the walls. The remainder of the complex, which is not connected to the Grand Palais, was designed by Jean Nouvel, Christian de Portzamparc and Jean-Marie Duthilleul.

Of the remaining architects, Libeskind aroused huge controversy by his design for the extension to the Victoria and Albert Museum, London, but presently is best known for his work on the Jewish Museum, Berlin, Germany, 1989–96. Eisenman's single major building to date has been the Wexner Center for the Visual Arts, Ohio State University, Columbus, Ohio, 1982–89; he has disavowed the validity of deconstructivism, using a computer morphing technique to explore what he terms fluid architecture.

The seventh, and one of the most radical of the exhibitors, was the Austrian Coop Himmelblau group, whose extreme designs question every aspect of traditional architectural geometry. The group's abilities are no more clearly expressed than in the pavilion later designed for the Groninger Museum, Groningen, the Netherlands, 1990–94, for which they collaborated with Michele de Lucchi and Philippe Starck. The Museum is situated on the Verbindingskanaal, astride a busy footbridge which connects the railway station with the centre of the city.

The 1980s also gave us the vigorous stream of high-tech architects led by Richard Rogers, Norman Foster and Renzo Piano, all designers who shared a commitment to the poetics of structure coupled with transparency and technology. The *Centre National d'Art et de Culture Georges-Pompidou* (Pompidou Centre), Paris, 1977, was the first building of note in the genre, followed by the Lloyds Building, London, 1978–86, by Rogers. This picturesque techno-romantic building, like the Pompidou Centre, is turned inside-out, with ducts, tubes and mechanical services sited externally. In place of a central core servicing the many floors was a vertical atrium that provided a new vision of the workspace ready for the coming age of electronic business. This was followed by Foster's Hong Kong and Shanghai Bank, Hong Kong, 1979–85, an essay in light, space and elaboration of detail that idealized technology, a strong counter-expression to the postmodernist packaged skyscrapers. Foster sited the main structural piers at the corners of the building, rather than at the centre of the building, which would have been more usual. The building sits on *pilotis*, over a pedestrian precinct at ground level, from which escalators rise through a slung glass membrane before emerging into the atrium.

Renzo Piano had moved on from his work in Paris; in his museum for the de Menil Collection, Houston, Texas, 1981–86, he used a slender steel frame to support an aluminium superstructure that holds a series of ferro-cement 'leaves' used to filter solar heat and glare. The result may be described as high-craft rather than high-tech, as these elements have a functional reason for being on the exterior of the structure. Nevertheless the high-tech idiom remained very popular.

Variations were soon to be seen; for example, Stansted Airport Terminal, Essex, 1981–91, by Foster, where a superstructure

Above, right and left: *Lloyds of London Building, 1986, by Richard Rogers. It epitomises the ideal of the modern movement by being absolutely a machine for working in. This deep-plan building is lit from an internal atrium, with much of its construction and the technological apparatus of climatic control on outward show* Facing page: *the Euralille complex, 1990–94, overseen by Rem Koolhaas, including the interior of the TGV station,* top right, *designed by Jean-Marie Duthilleul; the Crédit Lyonnais tower by Christian de Portzamparc and Claude Vasconi straddling the undulating 500 m (1,640 ft) long roof of the station,* top left; *front and side views of the 155,000 m² (1,668,420 sq ft) commercial centre, by Jean Nouvel,* centre left, above and below; *and,* bottom, *Rem Koolhaas' Grand Palais, a 50,000 m² (538,200 sq ft) convention centre*

The Hongkong & Shanghai Bank Headquarters, 1979–85, by Norman Foster Associates, is one of the key buildings of the twentieth century, displaying invention, technical innovation and architectural ability of a very high order. Almost every important element of the Bank HQ was designed and developed from scratch in collaboration with factory-based specialists, in effect reuniting the architect directly with the tools of building

Left: *photographed from the Botanic Gardens (south west)*

Right: *the Bank as seen from the east, with the Bank of China in the foreground*

Below: *the de Menil Collection, Houston, Texas, 1986, by Renzo Piano Building Workshop, is one of the best new galleries of the decade with its roof of 'leaves' of thin ferro-cement, suspended from an aluminium frame, that span the entire length of the building and act as light baffles to derive the maximum light without allowing direct sunlight into the gallery*

of parasol roofs floats on structural service columns, 'trees' with their trunks embedded in the ground and branches splaying above. Renzo Piano's own airport innovation was the Kansai Terminal, Osaka Bay, Japan, 1988–94, a linear, transparent building of repeated standardized structural elements that consist of a tensile beam and glazed membrane of uneven curvature.

By the end of the 1980s high-tech had developed beyond a technical neutrality towards a structural expressionism that relied upon the dynamic accentuation of the elements of construction, and which was evident in the biomorphic bridges, stations and airports of Santiago Calatrava.

Right: *the airside wing gate lounge, Kansai International Airport, Osaka, Japan, 1988–94, by Renzo Piano Workshop. The wing is formed of a simple and quiet spine housing ancillary spaces; the boarding lounges are attached airside of this spine under the tapering roof curve where the skin metamorphoses into a simple glass and aluminium system. Responding to the decreasing scale, the structure, technically a shell, is articulated in members of fine dimensions relating to human perception. All the internal elements, including the boarding bridges, are organised and composed for transparency*

Below: *a structural service column, which starts as a compact 'tree' trunk in the floor, gradually branching out to support the floating superstructure of silvery parasol roofs that cover the Terminal Building, Stanstead Airport, Stanstead, Essex, 1981–91, by Norman Foster. The grid of steel trees that supports the lightweight, service-free roof (which was erected first so as to provide a waterproof enclosure for the construction of the concrete beneath) are at 36 m (118 ft) centres. All steel members are circular in section; each trunk has four steel columns, and four slender branches*

Left: *an aerial view of Kansai International Airport, which was built on a man-made island in Osaka Bay*

Below: *the landside view of Stanstead Passenger Terminal, where the roof is projected by one bay to make a porte-cochère*

Above: *the great bird-like arch of the Satolas Airport TGV station, Lyon, 1993, by Santiago Calatrava, is typical of this architect's exciting* *bridges and railway stations, utilising beautiful and organic forms reminiscent of the* art nouveau *style that introduced this volume,* *and that can be seen in the illustration,* below right, *of the main concourse and,* below left, *a concrete portal to a platform*

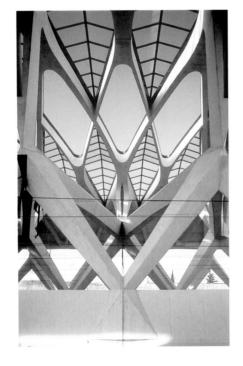

The 1990s

As the most imaginative designs of the late 1980s and early 1990s each took on the characteristics of a self-contained microcosm, a miniature world that encouraged interplay in a specific environment between its contents and the people who use it, their forms still continued to rely upon the major revolutions that had occurred earlier in the century. However these lines of continuity have grown ever more complex and diverse, with the resultant unexpected patterns and alignments that emerged in the face-off between individual dreams and collective ideals.

The last decade of the twentieth century has only just been consigned to history, and thus is far too close for any sensible categorisation; whether modernist, post-modernist, or deconstructivist, certainly these definitions have had their day, and we are faced with a kaleidoscope of styles that can, for the time being, be classified as:

- *relaxed modern*; pale stone, timber and glass as at the Pitcher & Piano public house, Newcastle-upon-Tyne, by Panter Hudspith; where the use of curves and rectangles gives a different composition from each viewpoint
- *metamorphic*; evocative, tactile structures such as the magnificently imaginative Guggenheim Museum, Bilbao, Spain, by Frank O Gehry

Above: *the Pitcher & Piano, Newcastle quayside, 1997, by Panter Hudspith*
Below: *the Guggenheim Museum, Bilbao, 1997, by Frank O Gehry, was the fruit of collaboration between the Solomon R Guggenheim Foundation and the Basque authorities, which is transforming the image of this ancient city*

Right: *Gehry's great titanium vessel used 33,000 sheets of titanium which weighed about 61 tonnes, and the cladding was applied by local shipbuilders. It is moored on the banks of the River Nervión in the heart of industrial Bilbao, and must already be considered one of the major buildings of the late twentieth century. Sitting beside a railway yard with a bridge crossing over it, the Guggenheim Museum houses nineteen galleries spread over three levels around a vast 55 m (82 ft) high central atrium that cuts through the heart of the building. The total floor space is 24,000 m² (258,336 sq ft), with 10,600 m² (114,098 sq ft) of exhibition area. The different forms of the Museum were modelled by Gehry, assisted by the computer program CATIA that had been developed by the French firm, Dassault, for fighter plane design*

- *neo-modern*; a renaissance of the pure white modern architecture of the 1920s and 30s, but updated by modern technology that makes the whole more hospitable and user-friendly, like the private house, Hampstead, London, 1998, by Rick Mather
- *neo-functionalist*; a rediscovery of the industrial aesthetic, as evidenced by the National Glass Centre, Sunderland, 1998, by Gollifer Associates
- *eco-tech*; an evolution of the high-tech that promotes energy-efficient natural cooling and ventilation, for example, represented by Feilden Clegg Bradley's New Environmental Office for the Building Research Establishment, Watford, 1995–96

In North America, specifically in southern California, there has been a resurgence of innovative architecture, prompted and promoted by Gehry, who has attempted to raise the level of architectural education through his involvement in the Southern California Institute of Architecture. This has been most noticable in relation to small-scale structures, where there has been a tendency towards whimsical sculptural forms, not necessarily related to the function of the space they enclose, but using materials and colours carefully selected to complement those forms and often dictated by cost parameters. Other architects such as Thom Mayne and his Morphosis practice, and Eric Owen Moss, who has done so much to rehabilitate Culver City, are part of this movement.

Also of note in California, but on an altogerther larger scale, is the San Francisco Museum of Modern Art, 1990–94, by Mario Botta, a massive building with a brick-veneer cladding. As the decade, the century and the millennium closed, however, a number of major projects were held over owing to financial considerations.

On mainland Europe, and France in particular, the situation has been very different. Although François Mitterand's stewardship ended in 1995, it was not until after he had created a lasting

Below: the entrance façade of the San Francisco Museum of Modern Art, 1990–94, by Mario Botta. There are no conventional windows to interrupt the brick façade, and so light is provided via the central sliced cylinder. The building costs were met mainly by private donations

Left: the Institut du Monde Arabe, 1981–87, by Jean Nouvel and the Architecture Studio, created a transparent oblong building (illustrated), united with a curved one that fronts onto the River Seine, around an inner court

The French monuments celebrated the Bicentennial of the French Revolution of 1789, and modernised the Parisian cultural infrastructure. The range of new buildings varied from I M Pei's Louvre pyramid, above left, *1983–88*, to Perrault's Grande Bibliothèque, above right, *1989–95, with its four towers resembling open volumns sited around a giant sunken garden.* La Grande Arche, right, *1981–87, was designed by Johann Otto von Spreckelsen to give a clear focus to the business district of La Défense, while Portzamparc's much-disputed scheme for the* Cité de la Musique *was in two halves, enclosing an open space which responds to both Tschumi's grid of follies of the* La Villette complex, *and the refurbished* Grande Halle. *The east complex, with the national instrument museum with Portzamparc's red folly on the Tschumi grid, can be seen* below left, *across the open space with lion fountain, and,* below right, *the Conservatoire, which is part of the west complex*

architectural legacy. His government had been responsible for numerous large-scale projects, particularly in the capital, Paris, which witnessed a variety of constructions. These had included Jean Nouvel's *Institut du Monde Arabe* and the perforated cube of *La Grande Arche de la Défense* by the Danish architect, Johan Otto von Spreckelsen, in 1987. These were followed by I M Pei's glass pyramid at the Louvre of 1988 and the completion, in 1995, of both Christian de Portzamparc's *Cité de la Musique*, and Dominique Perrault's *Grande Bibliothèque*.

In Germany there has been the huge redevelopment of Berlin's Potsdamer Platz, overseen by Renzo Piano and Christoph Kohlbecker, on a site of 68,000m² (731,952sq ft) in total. This included space for 620 residential units; 40,000m² (430,560sq ft) of retail outlets; a hotel with 350 rooms, 6 conference rooms and a ballroom; a CINEMAXX centre with 3,400 seats and 19 screens; a musical theatre; a variety theatre; an IMAX theatre and a casino.

Below: the Daimler-Benz Debis Tower, constructed on block C1 of the Potsdamer Platz redevelopment. The plot of land, in the shadow of the Berlin Wall, had been bought by Daimler-Benz in 1989, with the intention of building a headquarters building for its subsidiary company, Debis. Then then the Wall came down and Daimler found itself the owner of a prime piece of real estate

Right: *the rebuilding of the heart of Berlin, photographed from the Debis Tower (illustrated on the previous page) across the roof at the back of the building to the IMAX Theatre sphere, beyond which are two housing blocks, all of which are by Piano and Kohlbecker. To the left and just beyond the IMAX complex is the Hotel Grand Hyatt by José Rafael Moneo. In the lower left corner is the Musical Theatre, while running up the right hand side of the photograph from the bottom corner are offices by Arata Isozaki, a housing block by Lauber + Wöhr, then a second housing block and two office blocks, all by Richard Rogers*
Below right: *a plan of the same area, produced in June 1997, with the Debis Tower situated at the bottom (centre right), and the easily identifiable IMAX sphere, centre right*

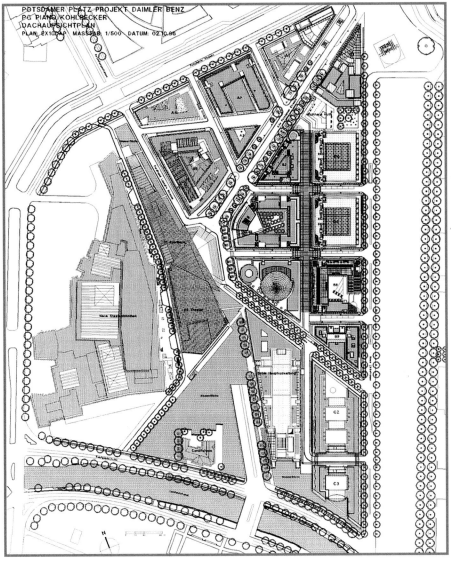

The international team of architects included Hans Kollhoff, Lauber + Wöhr (Ulrika Lauber and Wolfran Wöhr), José Rafael Moneo, Richard Rogers and Arata Isozaki. Norman Foster was busy refurbishing the Reichstag building to accommodate the relocation of the German Parliament to Berlin, at the same time.

Innovative architecture also continued to flourish in the Netherlands in the 1990s. Jo Coenen had already designed the successful Netherlands Architecture Institute building, Rotterdam, 1988–93. Alessando Mendini, together with a group of architects including Coop Himmelblau and Philippe Starck, designed the Groninger Museum, 1990–94. The building forms an artificial island in the Verbindingskanaal. A bridge which runs through the museum links the central train station to the town centre.

Above: *the Groninger Museum, Groningen, the Netherlands, 1990–94, designed by Alessandro Mendini with others, has at its centre the 60 m (197 ft) gold plastic laminate-covered treasury tower*

Left: *the Netherlands Architecture Institute building, Rotterdam, 1988–93, by Jo Coenen, which, like the more impressive Groninger Museum, is sited in a canal*

Architecture in Japan had flourished in the 1980s, with the emergence of talented architects such as Tadao Ando, Arata Isozaki, Toyo Ito and Fumihiko Maki. Although they produced such fine work as the Chikatsu-Asuka Historical Museum, Minami-Kawachi 1990–94, by Tadao Ando, the Shimosuwa Lake Suwa Museum, Shimosuwa-machi, Nagano, 1990–93, by Toyo Ito, and the Kirishima Concert Hall, Aira, Kagoshima, 1993–94, by Fumihiko Maki, perhaps the most outstanding building of the period in Tokyo is the Tokyo International Forum, 1989–96, by Rafael Viñoly, an enormous 130,000m² (1,399,320sq ft) complex located close to the Tokyo JR station on the site of the former Tokyo City Hall. This expensive monument to the Japanese building boom of the 1980s era and boasts the largest theatre in Tokyo. When the boom turned to bust, many developers found themselves overstretched in an area where by now there was an overcapacity.

Among other notable buildings elsewhere in Japan, two hotels capture the imagination: the Kyocera Hotel, Kagoshima,

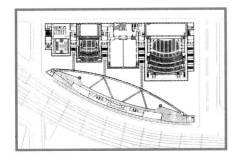

Above: *a plan of the Tokyo International Forum, 1989–96, by Rafael Viñoly, which includes a large glass hall that traces the curve of the adjacent railway track. The hall is one of the most spectacular internal spaces to have been created anywhere in the world in recent times, measuring 191 m (626 ft) in length by 30 m (98 ft) wide and soaring to a height of 57 m (187 ft). A screen of trees is planted between the glass hall and the more block-like forms of the convention centres and theatres at the top of the plan*

Far right: *the completed Petronas Towers and* right, *the site plan;* below, *the Sea Hawk Hotel*

by Kisho Kurokawa, and the 1052-room Sea Hawk Hotel and Resort Centre, Fukuoka, 1991–95, by Cesar Pelli. Pelli also designed one of the most breathtaking buildings of the century, Malaysia's twin Petronas Towers, Kuala Lumpur, 1991–97, Phase 1 of the Kuala Lumpur City Centre Project. These mighty towers, which are set in a development area of some 45ha (111 acres), stand 451 m (1,480 ft) high, making it the tallest building in the world. The 88 storeys above ground are linked by a 58 m (190 ft) long panoramic skybridge at the forty-first and forty-second floors, a height of 171 m (561 ft). In addition, there are four storeys below ground. The floor area of each tower is 214,000 m² (2,303,496 sq ft) and the external cladding is of stainless steel. The windows are protected by overhanging sunscreens, designed to shelter the interior from the tropical sun.

One of the largest mosques in this predominantly Muslim country is housed within the building, as well as the extensive offices and a retail centre. The standard security cameras and door-entry controls required 685 km (425 miles) of cables, but this intelligent double skyscraper also has 600 voice and data communications points and movement inside the building is tracked by monitoring the use of smart cards in the readers. The total capacity is for 20,000 people; there is parking for 10,000 cars, and a public park.

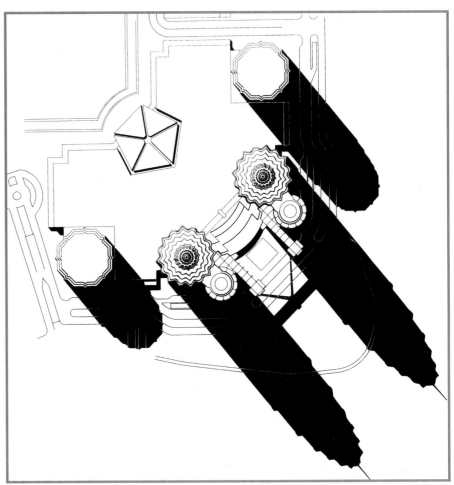

Chapter Two

Homes and Housing

The single-family dwelling

AT THE DAWN OF THE TWENTIETH CENTURY, both art and architecture everywhere were in the middle of a small stylistic revolution in the form of *art nouveau*, a style which discarded all of the characteristics of the previous century. Although it was a short-lived development in itself, its impact was profound and far-reaching.

Work in Europe early in the new century, particularly in Germany and in Austria, subsequently began to explore and to utilise new materials and forms. By the outbreak of the First World War, these already precluded the addition of earlier decorative elements, including those recently developed by the *art nouveau* designers, as architects stripped away applied decorative forms and colours in favour of an austerity of line and mass to give a purer form. Thus before the War began, the creative architectural role of Germany had been to develop the expressionist movement, which was to prove yet more powerful and influential.

Meanwhile in America Frank Lloyd Wright was beginning

Facing page: *Nirwana apartment building, Den Hague, the Netherlands, 1927, by Johannes Duiker, heralded the availability of new standards of comfort for the average resident during the interwar years*

Below: *the house for Mr W H Winslow, River Forest, Illinois, 1893–94, was one of Frank Lloyd Wright's first commissions after entering private practice earlier that year*

Above: *the house for Truus Schröder, Prins Hendriklaan 50, Utrecht, 1923–24*
Below: *the upper floor plans with screens closed (above), and open (below) for Rietveld's Schröder House, which was designed as a family dwelling, situated at the end of a suburban row*

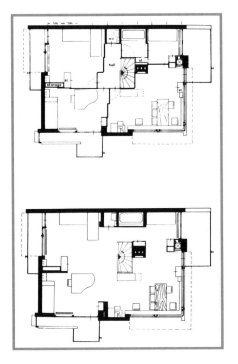

his career in Chicago with those highly-influential houses which were derived from the indigenous wooden style of the early settlers. This modern manner was established by the 1920s among the *avant-garde* as the future pattern of all buildings, including the private house, and it was to become the badge of the creative architect in North America and even in Europe.

The international style, with its distinctively rectilinear treatments, was born of the modern style in the 1930s. It came to dominate until well after the Second World War, but as more architects became dissatisfied with the restrictions that it imposed, eventually there was a reaction against it in the 1960s. The result was a new approach to domestic building, which made available a greater range of single-unit housing than had ever been dreamed of before. This style later became known as postmodernism.

Although architecture has always evolved and developed, perhaps this has continued at a greater speed and on a much wider scale in the twentieth century than ever before. By the 1980s, therefore, domestic building style had became high tech.

The buildings

One admirable example of the character of the modern movement is the Schröder house, Utrecht, the Netherlands, 1924, by Gerrit Thomas Rietveld. It is also the most famous of Rietveld's buildings. Like the designer's Red-Blue chair, which was closely associated with the design of the *de Stijl* movement, it has become a cult icon although it is a surprisingly small, semi-detached property at the end of a row. Mrs Schröder was closely involved with the design of her home (which is an entirely revolutionary building), particularly with the interior. Sliding screens vary the layout on the first floor, while the ground floor's interpenetrating cubicles include much intricately built-in furniture.

Walther Gropius designed houses for the staff of the Bauhaus, Dessau, in 1926. They were simple, stark and firmly based on modern rectilinear forms.

Le Corbusier built three of his most significant structures during the formative years of the modern movement: the Maison La Roche, Paris, 1923; Villa Stein, Garches, 1926–28, and Villa Savoye, Poissy, 1928–31, all of them works which fully realise the expression of the modern style in house-building terms.

A gallery was included at the Maison La Roche in order to display the owner's extensive collection of modern paintings. This room, together with the triple-floor height of the reception hall, works wonderfully with the disposition of the walls and the large windows to open up the interior. The whole evokes a controlled organisation of space, more so than in Rietveld's Schröder house, and more in line with the emerging modern movement evident in

Above:
Gerrit Thomas Rietveld's de Stijl *style icon, the Red-Blue chair*

Below: Pavillon de L'Esprit Nouveau *at the* Exposition Internationale des Arts Décoratifs et Industriels Modernes, *Paris, 1925, by Le Corbusier and Pierre Jeanneret was intended as the prototype for a modular living unit for villa apartment blocks*

Above: *a street of standardized houses for workers, designed by Walter Gropius between 1926–28*

Below: *the exterior of Villa Stein (Les Terrasses), Garches, near Paris, 1926–28, by Le Corbusier, and,* bottom, *an internal view of the first floor*

the Bauhaus staff houses. Le Corbusier did embrace the *de Stijl* aesthetic of Rietveld, however, within the organisation of his own geometrical schemes at both Garches and Poissy.

Villa Stein at Garches, which remains the most complete of Le Corbusier's masterpieces of house design, is laid out on a rectangular plan. The entire structure is supported on sixteen reinforced-concrete columns and the side walls are slung on long cantilevered members, a technique which provided tremendous freedom in the disposition of internal spaces. On the ground floor are the servants' quarters and garages, on the first floor is the large central living area, and on the top floor there is a terraced garden.

Villa Savoye is similar in plan, but its original setting was in an open field where it sat, majestically independent, on a flat plane. Again the first floor contains the living area and the second floor a roof garden, while the ground floor has a guest room added at one end. The ramp, already used in the studio wing of Villa La Roche, reappeared as a more central feature at Villa Savoye.

If the defining forms of European house building of the period were the houses of Le Corbusier, then Frank Lloyd Wright was his American counterpart. Wright's productive years spanned the most explosive expansion in American history. When he was born in 1867 the USA was home to 38 million people, of whom just one-quarter were city dwellers. When he died in 1959, there were no fewer than 180 million inhabitants, of whom almost three-quarters lived in cities.

Frank Lloyd Wright spent much of his time in California between 1917 and 1924, where he designed a number of important houses. There he used a new building process, which he called his textile block system, a name derived from the steel network that he

Above: *three typical Prairie Houses designed by Frank Lloyd Wright for the developer, Mr E C Waller.* Top, *with a hip-roof,* centre, *with a flat roof, and,* bottom, *with a gable.*
Wright had developed the Prairie House, a new type of dwelling, during his formative years which had culminated at the turn of the century. Its début had started an international revolution that continued to reverberate throughout suburbia for most of the new century. It offered an open spatial plan, a unified decorative scheme, and a reverence for family life, with a varity of solutions to suit differing clients, budgets, and sites

Right: *Storer House, Los Angeles, 1923, by Frank Lloyd Wright*

used. The more lavish of these was the Storer House, Hollywood Boulevard, Los Angeles, 1923, which used a split-level plan. Wright also designed all of the furniture and fittings in the house, but his previous design for the Millard House, Pasadena, 1923, also known as La Miniature, had even better detailing.

Although elements of the international style can be detected in his houses of the 1920s, it is unquestionably his personality that dominates the structures. Another of his most evolved works during this period was Taliesin III, Spring Green, Wisconsin, rebuilt from 1925 onwards following a bad fire, and still partly under construction when Wright died 34 years later. He created there one of the finest rooms of his career, a living room of many spaces all flowing together under the great central roof-ceiling. Here too were many of the most characteristic elements introduced by Wright to domestic architecture: a series of roof levels, some high and lofty, others low and sheltering sitting areas; a wide mix of materials and textures, including stone from the Wisconsin hills, natural wood and subtly-coloured plaster, and a catalogue of built-in furniture. At the heart of the house was a large rocky fireplace with a huge boulder used as a lintel, onto which a ray of light would play from a strategically-placed skylight.

Wright came close to bankruptcy when he was unable to meet his mortgage obligations on Taliesin III, and the banks foreclosed. The only way to save Taliesin was for Wright to incorporate himself and sell shares in his potential earning power to his wealthy friends. This he did, and the Taliesin Fellowship was founded; for a time, the building was used to house his architecture students, who also had to work the farm while studying.

The building of the Hollyhock House, Los Angeles,

California, 1920, a slightly earlier Wright house of this period, was overseen by Rudolph Michael Schindler, who had joined Wright's office in 1918. Schindler remained in Los Angeles, where he set up in practice separately. His own most famous building of the period was the Beach House, using poured concrete, where the house was raised on five free-standing piers with the prefabricated living space hung from the frames by means of steel rods.

Schindler had been born in Vienna just a few years earlier than Richard Neutra, who was a dedicated modernist and a strong propagandist of an architecture for the machine age. He in turn moved to America, and met Wright, who offered him a job at Taliesin. Neutra moved to Los Angeles in 1925, where he formed a partnership with Schindler. Dr Lovell, a health exercise practitioner, asked Neutra to design a home for him in 1927, that would also provide space for his professional apparatus. The Lovell House, Hollywood Hills, 1927–29, was the outcome. Built dramatically over a canyon, it not only made Neutra's reputation but is also regarded as having brought the international style to America. The original building was supported on shuttered concrete *pilotis* with cores of 10 cm (4 in) square steel posts.

Private house commissions became far fewer in the early 1930s in America and many architectural practices suffered as a direct result of the Depression. Wright built the conservative Willey House in 1934, and the Administration Building for the Johnson Wax Company in 1936, just before he went on to produce his most important and most famous buildings. He designed a house for Edgar J Kaufmann at Bear Run, Pennsylvannia, 1936, which was to become known around the world as Falling Water. This building, which was (and is) one of the most dramatically

Left: *the Edgar J. Kaufmann House (Falling Water), Bear Run, Pennsylvania, 1935–37, by Frank Lloyd Wright*

original new solutions in house design, re-established Wright as the pre-eminent creative architect of the era.

The house was built, indeed cantilevered, over a waterfall. Here Wright made his most poetic statement, and created the most complete edifice of his romantic beliefs. All of the ancient elements are used to build a temple dedicated to nature: the rocky ledge on which the house rests, the massive boulder that is allowed to penetrate the floor of the living area to form the hearth, the fire at the centre of the house, the waterfall below and the emphatic horizontal lines of those great sweeping cantilevers.

The house, which is simple by Wright's standards, is a geometrical composition of the concrete horizontals played against the vertical stone planes. It avoids boxiness, although many visitors are taken aback by its relatively modest size, as all interior corners dissolve into glass and all interior spaces extend across broad balconies and into the landscape. This wild romantic beauty has an almost universal appeal even today, regardless of whether or not the viewer is familiar with contemporary architectural theory. It has become the best-known modern house in the USA if not the world, with pictures of it being published everywhere.

Herbert F Johnson of the Johnson Wax Company commissioned Wright to design for him the house known as Wingspread, near Racine, Wisconsin, 1937. This large-scale building is similar in style to the much earlier Hollyhock House of 1920, with a central core and four wings. The master bedrooms are contained within one of the wings, while the others contain guest and childrens' rooms, service rooms, and garages. The tall living area, with its strange glass tower and clerestory roofing, has a period solidity that contrasts vividly with the gossamer-light quality achieved in Falling Water. During the two decades that

Below: *Wright's first Usonian House was completed in 1937 in Madison, Wisconsin, and is known as the Herbert Jacobs House*

followed, Wright was to lay the foundation for much modern domestic architecture in America in his so-called Usonian Houses.

The first of the Usonian Houses was designed by Wright and was constructed in 1937. These houses had walls of wooden sandwich construction and flat roofs of crossed wooden beams. Essentially they were a more modern version of the Prairie House concept, offering practical and attractive means of living the American dream. Each had a car port, built-in furniture, an open kitchen, a central fireplace, a dual-level roof and integral radiant heating.

Although the manner had been imported into the USA by Neutra, and the international style was first named there as such, it continued to develop within Europe, and by the time of the outbreak of the Second World War had become the accepted form for 'modern' architectural commissions. At the theoretical level the ideological battle had been won, so that architects could use this modern idiom which was the accepted solution for the future, able to serve every need and exploit every technological advance.

In reality, however, this ideal was widely diluted, and subverted beyond recognition. There was much jerrybuilding, with urban development throughout Europe creating a ribbon effect around major cities as row upon row of detached and semi-detached houses spiralled outwards from the city centres. Many of the innovations to be found in housebuilding were, as ever, naturally to be found in the homes that architects built for themselves, rather than in the traditional wood and brick boxes built to the economy of scale necessary to house the masses.

Erich Mendelsohn built for himself a large house at Grunewald, near Berlin, Germany, 1929–30, situated in its own extensive grounds. It showed all the characteristics of the international style; strong horizontal emphasis, linked fenestration, a flat roof

Below: *Erich Mendelsohn's own house, Grunewald, near Berlin, 1929–30*

Above: *this bungalow at Whipsnade, 1934, by Bernard Lubetkin and Tecton, had tightly-disciplined curved aerofoil forms*

Above: *house for Dr van der Vuurst de Vries, Waldeck Pyrmontkade 20, Utrecht, 1927–28, by Gerrit Rietveld*

Right: *High and Over, Amersham, Buckinghamshire, 1929–30, by Amyas Douglas Connell*

Below: *Sun House, Hampstead, London, 1935, by Maxwell Fry with Walter Gropius*

and the whole was starkly white, devoid of all applied decoration.

Mendelsohn emigrated to Britain in 1933, while Gerrit Rietveld continued to build upon the success of his Schröder house. He completed a number of dwellings in the Netherlands, also designing much of their furniture, during the 1930s.

In Finland, Alvar Aalto designed his own house and studio near Helsinki, 1935–36. He, too, also designed much of the furniture, specializing in the use of bentwood and laminated woods. In the true Finnish tradition, he also used wood structurally wherever possible, extensively on the façade of his own house, and even more liberally in the design of Villa Mairea, Noormakku, 1937–38. This building, which is based on a rectangular plan and is a summer house, is regarded as his finest domestic work.

The first fully-developed example of the modern style did not appear until 1930 in Britain. This was Amyas Connell's High and Over, Amersham, Buckinghamshire, which is Y-shaped in plan, developed out of a hexagonal core. At ground level the two short arms of the Y house the living room and the library, with the dining room, kitchen and services located in the longer arm. Each of the three arms may be opened, by the use of sliding double screens, to give access to the central hexagon. The other three sides of the hexagon give access to the entrances and the staircase.

Walter Gropius was also working in Britain in 1934, and in partnership with Maxwell Fry built the Sun House, Hampstead, London, 1935, among others. He did much to champion the case for modern architecture in a country where the architectural establishment was reluctant to experiment.

Meanwhile, Erich Mendelsohn had joined the practice of the Russian architect, Serge Chermayeff, and together they were commissioned to design an important house for a Mr Cohen at 64 Old Church Street, Chelsea, London, 1936. This domestic structure had strong overtones of their influential entertainment building, the De La Warr Pavilion, Bexhill-on-Sea, East Sussex, 1935. The latter had been commissioned two years earlier by the local council through an open competition under the auspices of the Royal Institute of British Architects, and a specifically modern solution was implied in the competition brief. It is technically remarkable chiefly for its welded steel frame. This was designed by the structural engineer, Felix Samuely, who had worked with Mendelsohn in Germany, as a lower-cost alternative to the original reinforced-concrete design.

Chermayeff's most successful work in England was his own house at Halland, Sussex, which followed in 1938. This open-plan arrangement has a long glass-fronted façade, which provides an immensely light interior. It occupies two storeys and makes extensive use of wood. Chermayeff emigrated to the USA in 1940.

Ludwig Mies van der Rohe had already gone to America, where he was the Director of the School of Architecture, Armor Institute, Chicago (which later became the Illinois Institute of Technology), from 1938. There, he grew to become one of the most powerful voices in modern architecture. His first house in America was built some 80 km (50 miles) west of Chicago at Plano, Illinois, 1945–50, for Dr Edith Farnsworth. It is a single glass box measuring 23.5 x 8.5 m (77 x 28 ft) and supported on a steel frame clear of the ground. It has a service area at its core, which provides a permanent dividing element, allowing a flexible separation of the remaining space. It was intended as a weekend retreat, set in isolated splendour in wooded countryside, and has a simple quality of truth in its construction. In this domestic pavilion the roof, floor and platforms are supported by the steel frame, and the whole structure rests on eight I-beams.

Above: *64 Old Church Street, Chelsea, London, 1936, and* below, *the staircase leading to the balcony and sun roof, De La Warr Pavilion, Bexhill-on-Sea, East Sussex, 1934–35, both by Erich Mendelsohn and Serge Chermayeff*

Left: *the Farnsworth House, Fox River, Plano, Illinois, 1945–50, by Ludwig Mies van der Rohe* Below: *Walter Gropius' own house, Lincoln, Massachusetts, 1939, with Marcel Breuer*

The Glass House in New Canaan, Connecticut, 1951, designed by Philip Johnson for himself, is an open-frame glass box; its circular brick service core is one-third along its length, but otherwise the concept is similar to that of the Farnsworth house although it was completed before the latter. Johnson had secured the original invitation to Mies van der Rohe to live in the United States, and commissioned furniture designs from him. However, it

Right: *the kitchen end of the Glass House, New Canaan, Connecticut, 1951, by Philip Johnson for himself*
Below: *an early work at Angmering, Sussex, 1936, by Marcel Breuer with F R S Yorke, in the international style*

Above: *the first Maison Jaoul, Neuilly, Paris, 1951–55, by Le Corbusier*
Below: *the second of the Jaoul houses, Neuilly, Paris, 1954–56, by Le Corbusier*

appears that Mies van der Rohe considered the design of the Glass House to be derivative and the detailing to be coarse, and that some time after it was built he and Johnson ceased to co-operate.

A first-generation student at the Weimar Bauhaus, Marcel Laiko Breuer, worked briefly in Britain with Francis Reginald Stevens Yorke, 1935–37. Walter Gropius, who had already moved to the USA from Britain, then invited Breuer to join him at Harvard, Cambridge, Massachusetts. They designed Gropius' house together in 1939, at Lincoln, Massachusetts, creating an early example in the eastern USA of the international style. They made extensive use of timber, helping to lend a different and softer character to the building, although it was reinforced with some steel members. In 1947 Breuer built his own house in New Canaan, Connecticut, using wood for both the cladding and for the structure of the living accommodation, with brick construction for the domestic services.

As Europe was otherwise engaged during the 1940s, the prime developments at the leading edge of architecture were in America. Richard Neutra designed the Kaufman House, Palm Springs, California, 1947, and Charles Eames built two Case Study Homes. These, sponsored by the magazine *Arts and Architecture*, used standard units that were available, assembled by Eames so as to show a wider potential for their use. José Luis Sert, another immigrant to America, opened a practice in Cambridge, Massachusetts, in 1955, building his own house there three years later. It was a further development of the rectilinear style, although not on a large scale.

Architects were beginning to find sufficient commissions again in Europe by the late 1950s, though the best examples are from the established practitioners such as Rietveld and his van Dantzig House, Santpoort, the Netherlands, 1959–60.

Throughout the 1950s and into the 1960s the major creative leader of the purest form of the international style was Le Corbusier, who began to search for a more relaxed attitude. He turned away from the stark white boxes on stilts to seek a new form of architecture, and in 1952 he built the first of two houses for the Jaoul family at Neuilly, Paris, France. Both this and the second home, completed in 1956, were in brick, concrete and wood, rough-hewn and sculptural in feeling, with strong dominating horizontal courses in concrete.

Also in Paris, Alvar Aalto built Maison Carré, Bazoches-sur-Guyonne, 1956–59, for an art dealer. It reversed the practice of the international style by making the art gallery the central focus and grouping the living quarters grouped around it.

Robert Venturi's book, *Complexity and Contradictions in Architecture*, 1966, identified a growing unease with the tenets of the basic international style, its variants and offshoots, largely initiating the next stylistic revolution in the United States of the 1960s.

Left: *Vanna Venturi House, Chestnut Hill, Philadelphia, 1962–64, by Robert Venturi for his mother*

Venturi's new ideas for architectural design had already been investigated in the building of his mother's house in Chestnut Hill, Philadelphia, 1962–64, and in the Guild House, a home for the elderly, also in Philadelphia, 1965. The house on Chestnut Hill is on two storeys, with a symmetrical façade. The entrance is very wide and deep-set; the pediment above it is pierced by a wide vertical slice that goes back to the depth of the entrance below.

Venturi was not the only architect to experiment with a developing style; another example is Herb Green's own self-constructed wooden shelter, Prairie House, Norman, Oklahoma, 1961. Sea Ranch, Gualala, Sanoria County, California, 1965, is a prototype condominium complex by Charles Moore of Moore, Lyndon, Turnbull, Whitaker. Some 320 km (200 miles) north of San Francisco, this group of buildings clusters on the side of a cliff. It was designed to evoke the pioneer homesteads of the old West, and each individual unit has a view overlooking the Pacific.

Other American houses of the 1960s in a modernist

Below: *Prairie House, Norman, Oklahoma, 1961, by Herb Green; a fanciful rendition in wood of a huge buffalo form, analagous to Frank O Gehry's more abstract ship alongside the port area of Bilbao for the Guggenheim Museum, 1997*

Above: *the Smith House, Darien, Connecticut, 1965–67, by Richard Meier*

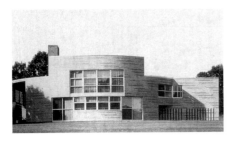

Above: *a view of Brant House, Greenwich, Connecticut, 1971, by Robert Venturi, showing the bulging façade. The diagonal texture of the green-glazed blocks on the façade helps to break up the symmetry. The entrance to the house is via the sunken garage, which is to the right of the photograph*
Below: *Venturi's 1978 house, built at New Castle, Delaware*

vernacular include Charles Gwathmey's own house and studio at Amagansett, New York, 1967. Here the combinations of solids, voids and angles show a more controlled organisation than in Moore's Sea Ranch condominium, though it still relies on the tradition of American building practices in its extensive use of wood; even the narrow exterior panelling is white-painted wood.

This was not a feature of Richard Meier's first commissioned house, the Smith House, Darien, Connecticut, 1965–67, which, with its hallmark white of the international style, is clearly derived from early Le Corbusier. Meier substituted a reinforced concrete structure with one of steel and brick with some decorative wood, whether because he was making a play on Corbusian style or as his contribution to extending further solutions in this idiom. The same could be said of Michael Graves who appears to have taken similar liberties in the design of his Hanselmann House, Fort Wayne, Indiana, 1967.

A maturing and an expansion of these new directions of the 1960s came as the restraints of the international style rapidly disappeared during the 1970s. Graves and Meier, together with Gwathmey, were among the designers represented at the Conference of Architects for the Study of the Environment (CASE) symposium, 1969, the others being Peter Eisenman and John Hejduk. An affiliated exhibition was held at the Museum of Modern Art, New York in that year. These architects, hitherto unknown on the international scale, were called the New York Five following their publication *Five Architects*, 1972, which set out the principles of the work in the exhibition.

In addition to these newly-recognised architects and their white houses, there remained the influential Robert Venturi. He designed the Brant House, Greenwich, Connecticut, in 1971, with a glazed and coloured brick asymmetrical façade. The setting and the layout of the house evoked a 1930s version of an English country house, as did those of the Weinstein House, *Old Westbury*, Long Island, New York, 1969–71, by Richard Meier. Here, Meier used a larger-scale winged plan, while his later Douglas House, Harbor Springs, Michigan, 1974, is a dramatic work which owes much to its setting on a steep wooded hillside.

Graves based his Snyderman House, Fort Wayne, Indiana, 1972, on a cubic volume, much like his earlier Hanselmann house nearby. Here, however, he more clearly demonstrates the Five's interest in thinness and the interaction of planes, perhaps in reaction against the blocky concrete of the international style.

Gwathmey's slightly later white house of the era is the Haupt Villa, 1977–78, built quite near to his own house in Amagansett. The high water table locally and the resultant building regulations posed particular problems, for which he made clever provision.

White gave way to colour, scale increased with affluence,

classical elements began to reappear and became more evident as the cube increasingly became the starting point rather than the end product. Venturi used classical elements; humorously misplaced though they were, in designing a house at New Castle, Delaware, in 1978, that was quite different from the Brant House. As ever, the architect was not always utterly trusted and allowed a free hand; the wishes of clients had to be considered but nonetheless many of the frontiers of architecture had been pushed forward by designs for the architects' own houses.

Towards the end of the decade other architects were beginning to cause excitement, particularly Mario Botta in Europe. He gradually evolved a distinctive personal style in a series of houses that were all sited on the hillsides overlooking Lake Lugano, or on the outskirts of industrialised villages, in the Swiss canton of Ticino. His style made great use of bold rectangles, cylinders, and symmetrical planes with slots for circulation, in an attempt to fit the building to the surrounding topography. Early examples included the Bianchi House at Riva San Vitale, 1971–73; those at Ligornetto, 1975–76, and Pregassona, 1979–80. These were followed by a wonderful array of individual residences such as the Medici House (known as Casa Rotonda) at Stabio, 1980–82, and others at Comano, 1981; Morbio Superiore, 1982–83; Breganzona, 1984–88; Vacallo, 1986–89, and Losone, 1987–89.

Three houses by Mario Botta, in his distinct personal style: top, *at Riva San Vitale, on Lake Lugano, Ticino Canton, Switzerland, 1971–73;* below left, *the north front; and,* below right, *the south front of the Medici House, known as Casa Rotonda, Stabio, Switzerland, 1980–82, and* bottom, *via Arbostra 27, Pregassona, Ticino Canton, Switzerland, 1971–73*

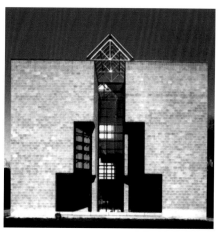

Buildings were being constructed elsewhere in the 1980s that were also better suited to their climate, place and landscape, embracing both social and technological change. The best of these also drew upon indigenous wisdom, such as the Ramada House, Tucson, Arizona, 1980, by Judith Chafee, who adapted ancient building techniques of the desert climate and combined them with a considered use of space and structure. The building is formed

Above: *the Koshino House, Hyogo, Japan, 1979–81, by Todao Ando, one of the architect's buildings of the period that were stripped down to essentials. His use of plainer, smooth-concrete walls, frames, vaults, glazing, and glass bricks created a sense of order, light and space*

Right: *the interior of the Koshino House*

like a protective parasol of wooden shading slats placed above the adobe substructure of whitewashed walls.

Tadao Ando was working to the same ends in Japan. Using modern western techniques and materials, he too attempted to restate the unity between house and nature that had been lacking so far in attempts to impose the international style upon the Japanese way of living. His buildings, such as the Matsumoto House, also known as the Wall House, at Ashiya, Hyogo, Japan, 1976–77, and the Koshino House, Hyogo, 1979–81, supplied a minimalist alternative to the visual chaos of modern urbanisation. They excluded the outside world by means of blank walls that opened up onto a sequence of passageways, rooms and courts, with light carefully controlled and directed to evoke a timeless peace and inner stillness.

This empathic adaptation to the individual environment was also becoming evident in those countries where traditional architecture had not kept pace with the changes in traditional society. In India, for example, there had been massive influxes into the cities of poor people from the country as they sought work, which resulted in vast squatter settlements in and around the main cities. Balkrishna Doshi did a great deal of city planning work in the 1980s, in particular submitting proposals for Indore, 1984, and Vidyadhar Nagar, a satellite city of 350,000 people sited close to the early eighteenth-century city of Jaipur, in 1986. His plan for Vidyadhar Nagar embodied ancient Hindu cosmological lore, coupled with modern energy conservation and the elaboration of several arrangements of dwellings based on the courtyard.

Doshi was able to put some of his visions into practice at his own house at Ahmadabad, which incorporated his studio. The building was formed from low parallel vaults rising from earth mounds and platforms traversed by channels of water. The interiors, like those of Judith Chafee's Ramada House, were half-buried in the ground, where likewise they would be better protected from the heat and dust. The vaults were constructed from ceramic tubes covered in concrete and broken white tiles, forming an insulation that helped to reduce the temperature in the hottest months. The glare of the sun was reduced by filtering light indirectly under hooded overhangs or through skylights, and the whole represented the architect's ideal of harmony between the individual, the community, and nature, a careful balance between modern architecture and vernacular form.

The innovation and profundity of the houses of Frank Lloyd Wright, which had begun the century in North America, had established a tradition of true individualism and innovative solutions for the single-family house. During the second half of the 1980s in North America, architects entirely dispensed with conventional traditional urban spaces ornamented with various kinds of classical figuration. Instead they exhibited a new vitality that confronted the mess of the inner-city sprawl head-on. The mood was championed by leading architects such as Frank O Gehry, who produced thought-provoking designs, often for extensions or remodelling to existing buildings. He juxtaposed carefully-considered solutions to disparate problems within a single building, that on the surface appeared to be an ad-hoc assembly of different elements.

Gehry's work had been developed from the Spiller House, Venice, California, 1979, via others that reflected their environment, such as the Norton House, also in Venice, 1982–84, and which used unusual combinations of materials such as concrete block, glazed tile, stucco and wooden logs. It also has a detached study, similar in appearance to the local lifeguard shelters, raised on a slender podium and with rope-controlled windows.

Above: *a sketch section showing the sunken rooms and the domed roofs of Balkrishna Doshi's house and studio, Sangath, which lies on the outskirts of Ahmadabad, 1979–81*

Left: *the Spiller House (behind and to the left of the white building on the right), Los Angeles, 1980, by Frank O Gehry. This unconventional residence formed part of the architect's anti-modernist protest*

His later buildings such as the Schnabel House, Brentwood, California, 1990, were produced along the way to his complete break with normal conventions, displaying the fractured geometry of an abstract sculpture to produce a contemporary work of art. This approach reached a more tactile conclusion in his Guggenheim Museum, Bilbao, 1991–97, a complex structure of interpenetrating walls, floors, ceilings and skylights clad in shining titanium. Nonetheless, this fantastical profusion of convex and concave planes is capable of evoking unexpected emotional responses as well as its visual association with its nautical setting.

The effect of this idiosyncratic architectural evolution is an inimitable structure, more personal in its origins, that lacks a social or ideological agenda yet where the form still follows the function, although in accordance with an individual, iconoclastic vision. The route towards fragmentation and abstraction is also evident in the works of the neo-modernist former New York Five members Richard Meier and Peter Eiseman, although their theories were essentially transmitted in the larger, non-domestic, commissions which they received.

Equally radical dwellings of the last decade of the twentieth century include the T-House, Wilton, New York, 1988–94, by Simon Ungers and Tom Kinslow, and two houses by Bart Prince. The T-House has a simple geometric structure of 6 mm (quarter-inch) oxidised nickel-chromium steel, with the living quarters below and a library, separated in the cross of the T, above.

Bart Prince built the Mead-Penhall residence, Albuquerque, New Mexico, 1992–93, as a low-cost dwelling that also drew upon modern materials, such as galvanised metal sheeting for the sides of the house. The Hight residence, Mendocino County, California, 1994–95, blends naturally into its surroundings while acting as a shield from the northerly winds. Here Bart Prince used glue-laminated beams and an undulating shingled cedar roof, evocative of the waves of the Pacific Ocean which it overlooks.

Above: *walls, ceilings and walkways that overlook the atrium of the Guggenheim Museum, Bilbao, 1991–97*
Below: *side and top elevations of the T-House, Wilton, New York*
Below right: *end elevations showing the undulating shingle roof of the Hight seaside house, Mendocino County, California*

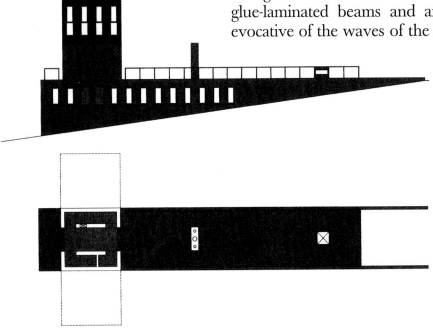

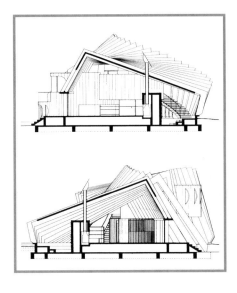

Multi-unit housing

Apartment blocks vary in size considerably, from very small groupings, perhaps of two-storey blocks, to the high-rise towers or skyscrapers that are now more familiar almost everywhere. In many cases, certainly within high-rise towers, the accommodation that is provided is uniform from storey to storey, having been designed on a floor arrangement that is then replicated to fill the given space in order to achieve economies of scale. It is thus the architect, rather than the individual inhabitant, who determines the layout of the individual housing units as well as the structure's single identity, and who imposes his personality on the building.

Left: *Kijk-Kubus, Overblaak 70, Rotterdam, by Piet Blom, built in the 1980s*

The many undistinguished blocks that scar our city skylines generally have been commissioned by commercially-driven clients (including publicly-funded bodies such as councils) with little consideration other than cost. It is unjust to blame the architect, who must work closely to a brief which describes the facilities to be provided, and within perameters which restrict the costs; also, frequently the architect is required by the town planners to observe restrictions dictated by the surroundings. Fortunately, not all of these criteria apply to all new housing all of the time.

During the twentieth century the continuing expansion of populations, although not at a uniform rate, increased the pressure on housing stocks. Whereas populations have tended to gather increasingly in urban centres, particularly as countries have developed, ever-changing social arrangements elsewhere have compounded the problem by exerting an ever-growing demand for single-occupancy apartments and single-parent family accommodation as a proportion of the general population.

Furthermore as housing demand increases, land prices rise also, and the most economical option for the developer is then to

Right: *Nirwana flats, Den Hague, the Netherlands, 1927, by Johannes Duiker, were based on American-style comfort*
Below: *the Doldertal Apartments, Zürich, Switzerland, 1934–36, by Alfred and Emil Roth with Marcel Breuer; these boxes on stilts are in the international style*

Unité d'habitation

Le Corbusier's Marseilles project is a vertical community of 18 floors. The 1,800 inhabitants are housed in 23 types of duplex (split-level) apartments. Common services include two 'streets' inside the building, with shops, a school, a hotel and, on the roof, a nursery, a kindergarten, a gymnasium and an open air theatre. The apartments were conceived as individual villas stacked in the concrete frame like bottles in a rack. It was completed in 1952 and two more *Unités* were built in France, one at Nantes and the other at Briey, while another was built in Berlin.

expand vertically rather than horizontally. Even in America, where land is relatively plentiful, in such great manufacturing centres as Chicago masses of manual workers needed to be within easy access of their place of work. Land became increasingly in short supply, which in turn increased population density.

High-rise domestic buildings had only became viable after the development of reinforced concrete in the previous century. It supplied the means for building them in the combination of tensile strength, derived from the steel, and compressive strength, derived from the concrete. The form and appearance of high-rise apartment blocks and other skyscraper buildings of the twentieth century is partially derived from the characteristics of reinforced concrete, one major limitation of which is that it is not easily decorated. Simple and stark in its early incarnations, it provided the basis for a new aesthetic, related to the abstractions of modern art.

The major protagonists of this modern movement, the international style, all participated in the design of multi-unit housing, but none of the major projects was completed until after the conclusion of the Second World War. The postwar building boom was ignited by Le Corbusier's *Unités d'habitation*, designed at the end of the 1940s. These self-contained living units were open at ground level, had shops between the accommodation levels for maximum access, and a kindergarten next to the roof garden.

The first of these is in Marseilles and comprises 337 apartments, but in all 23 different apartment layouts were used to accommodate a mix of differently sized families. It formed part of Le Corbusier's larger plan for massive urban developments which were embodied in his *La Ville Radieuse* (Radiant City), published in 1930–35. Le Corbusier's apartment blocks provided a new conception, the aim of which was to limit the urban sprawl.

While Le Corbusier was busy proselytising his ideas in the rebuilding of Europe, Ludwig Mies van der Rohe had settled in Chicago. There he embarked on the Lake Shore Drive Apartments, 1948–51, on the edge of Lake Michigan. These two adjacent blocks were unlike Le Corbusier's in that they did not attempt to provide for a complexity of residents and their needs. They were sited on a triangular lot and faced different ways, but otherwise the proportions of the 26-storey blocks were identical. This produced austere monoliths, typical of the modern rectilinear aesthetic, and their simple slab-like appearance was to become the template for a succession of apartment blocks that followed in the next 20 years.

By the 1960s, however, the American economy was flourishing, and a general dissatisfaction began to form against the dull and unoriginal appearance of the accommodation available. The development of postmodernism had relatively little impact on multi-unit housing, however, and its influence continued to be slight, being felt more strongly in other areas. Similarly there were to be few examples of high-tech designs in the apartment-block category, although the use of metal structures for porticos, porches and conservatories did slowly gain in popularity.

Europe had been in desperate need of extensive rebuilding works immediately after the First World War, and whereas in Britain there was a tendency to achieve this by building satellite towns of the Garden City type, on mainland Europe the tendency was to build higher. In Germany especially there was a demand for more spacious accommodation, with better facilities and services. The continental solution was to construct large apartment blocks on greenfield sites on the outskirts of the major cities. Inevitably this resulted in increased traffic congestion as the inhabitants of these blocks travelled to work in the city centres, and attempts to solve this problem only gave rise to further accommodation needs.

The Weißenhofsiedlung exhibition at Stuttgart, Germany, was organised by Ludwig Mies van der Rohe in 1927. Under his direction, 17 of the leading architects of the day, including Le Corbusier, Hans Poelzig, Hans Scharoun and Max Taut, were to create a model group of 21 houses and apartments. The intention was that these would be suitable for occupation by the middle classes, with villas bordering the estate next to the road.

Under his direction the team of architects achieved a harmonious overall stylistic unity. Mies van der Rohe himself designed the focal four-storey apartment block, which was in four main sections. Although the design had been hurriedly prepared, its layout set a pattern that was to be repeated time and again throughout the following decade, until the outbreak of the Second World War. The bold massing of the white blocks, open planning and machine-age details were to become the hallmarks of the international style.

Below: apartments on the Weißenhofsiedlung, Stuttgart, 1927, by Mies van der Rohe

Walter Gropius, who had been involved in the Stuttgart project, was appointed the leading architect for the building of the Siemensstadt Estate, near Berlin, in 1929–30. A team of the foremost architects was assembled once more, this time to create recreational and housing facilities for the workers of Siemens. Most successful here was Hans Scharoun's apartment block, which used curvilinear forms in a design that was less harsh than the straightforward rectilinear designs of Gropius. Significantly, it incorporated shops and services as well as apartments.

The Karl-Marx-Hof housing scheme was being built in Vienna at much the same time, 1928–30, under the direction of Karl Ehn, the city architect. A bold impressive sculptural exterior here denotes one of the best-known and most acclaimed housing schemes. It is grandiose but well laid out, and was based on high-density planning principles. By today's standards, it is defective as a settlement in the detailed planning of the flats, many of which are back to back and do not have the benefit of sunlight.

Above: an apartment block on the Siemensstadt Estate, 1929–30, by Hans Scharoun
Right: Karl-Marx-Hof, Vienna, 1928–30, by Karl Ehn, stretched for more than 800 m (half a mile), and contained 1,382 apartments, offices, laundries, green spaces, a library, and an out-patients' clinic
Below: High Point I flats, Highgate, London, 1933–35, by Berthold Lubetkin with Tecton. The building was a masterly achievement, built on a cross of Lorraine plan to maximise views across London and adapting Le Corbusier's white forms

The international style became established during the 1930s, and by the end of that decade it had achieved full international acceptance. The style provided an alternative for architects who were designing skyscrapers in North America that were not period reproductions; the buildings could be high and smooth, and the top could be flat because the building was so high that it was out of sight. Coupled with improved elevator technology, the style's ready acceptance enabled *high* to become *higher*, and although by far the majority of these buildings were for business activities, some were for apartments.

England lagged behind, however, continuing to concentrate

on single housing units, but a few apartment blocks did emerge. Ironically these included what was then the largest apartment complex in Europe at Dolphin Square, London, 1936. Designed by Cecil Eve and Gordon Jeeves, the block contains 1250 flats and covers 3.04ha (7.5 acres). It is ten storeys high with a steel frame, and faced in dull red brick with stone dressings. As well as a central garden, it included shops, a restaurant and a garage.

Perhaps better known are the two blocks of apartments, Highpoint I and Highpoint II, in Highgate, north London. The eight-storey Highpoint I apartment block, 1935, was one of the most successful buildings for the Tecton Group. This was one of the first teams of architects set up in Britain with a commitment to modern design. Its most influential partner was the Russian émigré, Berthold Lubetkin. These flats, with their discordant pair of caryatids supporting a *porte-cochère* inspired by Le Corbusier, gained an international reputation because of their fine finishes. Highpoint II, which followed in 1937–38, extended the estate by adding a further thirteen luxury dwelling units.

The Second World War interrupted building programmes worldwide, and when they recommenced they continued where they had left off, with the established international style. The only remaining established leading architect still to be practising in Europe by this time was Le Corbusier. His reputation was now such that he was freed to adopt a more expressive and emotional approach rather than the more rigorous, purist line being taught by Mies van der Rohe, who had been practising in the United States from 1938. Thus the current style, which had been international, diverged; one approach was followed in Europe, while the other came to dominate in America.

In Europe, Le Corbusier produced some of his finest works. He was invited to prepare a scheme for the rebuilding of the town centre of Saint-Dié in the Vosges mountains, 1945, and this project to house 30,000 people gave him the opportunity to extend his ideas yet further into the area of town planning. However, when this scheme was cancelled, he was deeply disappointed and circulated the drawings indiscriminately, as a result of which they became hugely influential in disseminating his ideas.

The *Unité d'habitation* at Marseilles, 1946–52, developed from this scheme, represented the fullest expression of the ideas concerning the complete environment that had been Le Corbusier's abiding preoccupation since the early 1920s. His use of reinforced concrete in this context exploited its inherent versatility; it permitted him a greater freedom of construction, in addition to its sculptural form and surface textural opportunities. Further apartment blocks followed, at Rezé-les-Nantes, 1952–54, in Berlin, 1956–58, at Briey-en-Forêt, near Metz, 1957–59, and at Firminy, near St Etienne, completed in 1968.

Not only was Marseilles an important design, but it

> **Other mid-century British apartment blocks**
>
> Alton Estate, Roehampton, Surrey, 1955–59, by London County Council Architects Department. A group of high rise blocks that overlook Richmond Park.
> Ham Common, Surrey 1958, by James Stirling and James Gowan. A development of two-storey blocks of apartments that combine the use of brick with exposed concrete beams.

Below: Unité d'habitation, *280 boulevard Michelet, Marseilles, 1946–52, by Le Corbusier*

Above left: *the façade of*
Unité d'habitation, *Briey-en-*
Forêt, France, 1957–59, by
Le Corbusier
Above right: *a corner of his*
second Unité *to be built, at Rezé-*
les-Nantes, 1952–54, showing
the shuttered concrete pilotis. *The*
influence of these buildings on
architecture was profound, and
elements of them, from the simple
béton brut *to* brise-soleil, *can*
be seen throughout the 1950s and
the 1960s

The language of
Le Corbusier

béton brut: literally, raw concrete.
Wooden shutters are used to contain
the wet poured concrete, which may
take on the grain of the shutter
timbers when they have been
removed. In England, the shutters are
known as form-work.
brise-soleil: a sun-break, used to shade
the window openings; now, frequently
an arrangement of horizontal or
vertical fins.
pilotis: the French term used by Le
Corbusier to denote the stilts, used as
foundation piles, to support his
buildings.

---

benefitted tremendously from being one of the most important public commissions of the time in Europe. Consequently the building was debated and dissected at length. Its radical design, its aesthetic qualities, its shortcomings, and every other detail were openly investigated and its many and varied architectural lessons eagerly learnt throughout the profession. The block was designed to be home to 1,600 inhabitants, refugees from the bombed-out port area of the city, and was originally planned as the first of four such blocks. The others, which were never built, were to be erected on neighbouring sites.

The *Unité d'habitation* building was the first large-scale project to be based on Le Corbusier's Modulor system, and his rendition of a human image that represents this is incorporated on one of the exterior walls. This measurement scheme for deciding harmonious proportions is basically a synthesis of the Golden Section ratio and an analysis of the proportions of the human body. The Golden Section has been used since ancient times in many cultures for buildings of all kinds. If a rectangle is divided into two unequal parts, so that their ratio to each other is the same as that of the larger part to the whole, this proportion cannot be precisely described mathematically but approximates to 8:13. Le Corbusier's Modulor Man is much more specifically described, but the combination of these two ideas became a determinant of his designs, and it can be seen in many of his later buildings.

It is raised on *pilotis* 7 m (23 ft) clear of the ground. The differently-sized apartments were designed to house a varying number of occupants, ranging from single individuals to families with five children. The overall size of the structure is 137 m (450 ft) long x 24.4 m (80 ft) wide and it rises to a height of 56 m (184 ft)

Far left: *Promontory Apartments, 5530 South Shore Drive, Chicago, 1949, by Mies van der Rohe, was the architect's first high-rise building after his emigration from Europe, and typical of the trend towards a simple style after the Second World War. They were designed to be cost-effective, with light-coloured brick panels and aluminium windowframes set into a reinforced-concrete frame emphasised by the projecting columns*

Left: *860–880 Lake Shore Drive, 1948–51, by Mies van der Rohe, two linked apartment buildings that provided the model for vitreous, rectangularly prismatic high-rise structures. They had a five-by-three bay plan; the north tower reveals its wider side to Lake Shore Drive and the south tower its narrower side. They dominated the international architectural landscape for 20 years*

being set in landscaped grounds extending to 3.6 ha (9 acres).

The Marseilles building uses the effect of shuttering as an essential decorative element, and during the later 1950s this became a fashionable treatment of concrete in Europe. It also represents Le Corbusier's fresh approach to the increased scale of communal housing, contrasting with the clean white surfaces of his prewar private villas. He also used concrete fins to break the surface into areas of grid pattern, and strong colours on the façades and in the internal corridors.

The divergent route of the international style was developing simultaneously in America, more specifically in Chicago on the shores of Lake Michigan. Here Mies van der Rohe's design philosophy was epitomised by his two tower blocks at 860 and 880 Lake Shore Drive, which were to dominate the design aesthetic in America until the 1960s. The international style had enabled architects to minimise costs by using expensive stone only to clad a steel or reinforced-concrete skeleton.

Mies van der Rohe had been unable to use the steel frame originally intended for the Promontory Apartments block, begun in 1946, owing to shortage of steel during the Korean war. Reinforced concrete was used instead, clad in light-coloured brick panels. The 20-storey blocks at Lake Shore Drive were built with a steel structure, were rectangular in plan, set at right angles to each other, and connected by a covered way. Steel I-beams bolted to the frame act as defining mullions to the glass, running from the first-floor level to the full height of the blocks.

The effect is one of a tall, simple box structure. Its open ground level, centralised lift shafts and service core were to become typical of the next two decades. Indeed, Mies van der Rohe's office

Other contemporary American apartment blocks

Price Tower, Bartlesville. Oklahoma, designed 1929, built 1953–56, by Frank Lloyd Wright. A combined office and apartment block for the H C Price Co, it is a small skyscraper of eighteen storeys with a cross-shaped spine supporting the building and from which all floors are cantilevered out.

Workers Housing Development, New Kensington, near Pittsburgh, Pennsylvania, 1941, by Walter Gropius. Designed to house defence workers, it was a low-cost enterprise comprised of wood-constructed buildings which all had open plan ground floors, but which never proved to be popular with their occupants.

Mill Creek I, Philadelphia 1952–53, by Louis Kahn. A group of three public-housing tower apartment blocks that create a sense of vertical unity.

Mill Creek II, Philadelphia 1959–62, by Louis Kahn. A two-storey housing block build adjacent to Mill Creek I from which they also contrast in both texture and colour.

Above: *the 15-storey Usk Street block in Bethnal Green, London, 1954, by Denys Lasdun*
Below: *the 19-storey Romeo apartment block, Stuttgart, 1957–59, by Hans Scharoun*

alone designed about 37 buildings of the type during that time.

The period of perhaps 25 years that follows is characterised by more stylistic cohesion for multi-unit housing; as resources were allocated to increased social housing, younger architects who had been trained in the styles of Le Corbusier and Mies van der Rohe were set to work, and their ideas cross-fertilised. Although the apartment block previously had not been the main type of housing in Britain, population pressure in most urban areas now made living in a flat socially acceptable. This changing social pattern fuelled the need, helping to stimulate an unprecedented frenzy of building both public-authority and commercial privately-developed apartment blocks.

Hindsight now suggests that by their design, in some cases these may have created as many social problems as they solved. The large-scale uniform developments by local housing authorities initially were thought to offer elegant solutions to the need for a socially stimulating environment. Sadly, in use their long balconied walkways and enclosed, lightless stairwells providing access to the apartments' front doors were transformed into sources of vandalism, violence and fear. Most authorities have been forced to reconsider this solution, and in recent years have carried out extensive rebuilding and refurbishment to mass-housing estates.

The difficulty of the urgent and increasing problem of providing a safe, secure low-income housing environment remains one of society as a whole, rather than the architect alone. The possible provision of government-subsidised mortgages to key workers in healthcare and law enforcement is merely a restoration in an altered form of the traditional subsidised tied housing for such workers, and is unlikely to yield any effect on new building.

It would be very wrong, however, to think that all of Britain's mid-century high-rise apartment blocks were dismal and abused. There were many well-planned successes which generally tended to be one-offs, each being too expensive an exercise to repeat. Undoubtedly these include the Usk Street block in Bethnal Green, London, 1954, by Denys Lasdun, who built a 15-storey structure which attempted to retain the social environment of the small Victorian houses that it replaced. The block consists of four maisonettes per floor on the lower levels, and single-room apartments higher up. The block was being refurbished with advice from the architect at the time of his death, although sadly it is no longer in local-authority ownership and the revitalised apartments and added penthouse will command premium prices.

Mainland Europe was proving rather more fertile ground for the development of apartment housing during the same period, ranging from the unusual Romeo and Juliet apartment blocks, Stuttgart, Germany, 1957–59, by Hans Scharoun, to the more rudimentary though imaginative blocks such as that on the Barrio Gaudí, Reus, Spain, 1964–72, by Ricardo Bofill. Scharoun's blocks at Stuttgart are part of a housing estate, and sit majestically on a hill. The Romeo block contains six apartments which are grouped around the central access on each of the 19 storeys, while the later Juliet block is built to a horse-shoe plan, creating irregular-shaped rooms, rising at its highest point to 12 storeys. Both blocks have unusually-shaped projecting pointed balconies.

Bofill's Reus building is designed to a far lower budget, and is arranged as a much freer cluster of concrete, brick and colour. He was responsible for some of the more imaginative and striking housing projects of the era, and was never afraid of using classical elements, though in often novel and misplaced ways and in unusual materials. He has a special liking for giant Doric orders which often scale the entire height of his multi-storey buildings,

Some of Ricardo Bofill's housing complexes: below left, *that at Barrio Gaudí, Reus, Spain, 1964–72;* below centre, *Walden-7, Sant Just Desvern, Barcelona, 1970–75;* below right, *Le Palais, Les Espaces d'Abraxas, Marne-la-Vallée, Paris, 1978–83, and* bottom, *the building at Le Viaduc, Saint-Quentin-en-Yvelines, Paris, 1974, where 74 apartments jut out into the lake*

lending an appearance of grandeur to fairly basic accommodation; however, these classical elements are often put to practical use, containing service lifts or staircases.

At this point a growing backlash was forming against modernism, which had been almost universally applied in the urban renewal of the 1960s. Furthermore, increasingly it was being blamed for disregarding human needs, for not blending in, and even for being an instrument of class oppression. The styles of many of the leading architects of the period metamorphosed in response, as they struggled to design more within existing contexts and precedents. At the same time, they were exposed to competition from young architects who had a fresh approach and who were beginning to receive major new commissions. The perception that one period of architecture was making way for another became widespread, as the architects who were regarded as postmodern were eagerly welcomed.

Bofill's contributions to the housing complexes at St Quentin-en-Yvelines, 1974, and Marne-la-Vallée, 1978–83, west and east of Paris respectively, are in marked contrast to his earlier work in Spain at Reus, or the transitional style of Sant Just Desvern. These new French towns were built around the capital after the Second World War, along with Evry, Melun Senart and Cergy-Pontoise, and were conceived on a monumental scale.

There were an enormous variety of forms in America during both the 1960s and 1970s; although basically the influence still came from Mies van der Rohe, other major immigrant architects were now in practice there. Gropius, Breuer, and Saarinen were all working within the modern movement, but in a new sophistication of the original aesthetic. This led many critics by the end of the 1970s to pronounce the death of modern architecture in the international style.

Above: *Lake Point Tower, Chicago, 1968, by Schipporeit-Heinrich Associates, which at 196.6 m (645 ft) on completion was the highest reinforced-concrete building in the world. Its flat-slab frame with a sheer wall core in the shape of a triangular prism constitutes a unique structural system*

Left: *Marina City, 300 North State Street, Chicago, 1964–67, by Bertrand Goldberg Associates, lies on the north bank of the river and is affectionately known as the corn cobs. The two 60-storey apartment towers are of concrete construction, in which the loads are carried mainly by cylindrical cores. The complex embraces 900 apartments (having pie shaped rooms that extend into rings of semi-circular balconies), garages (with the parking space arranged on a continuously rising helical slab through the first 18 floors), offices, a bank, restaurants, a gym, a marina, a television studio and a theatre*

Facing page: *Phase One, River City, 800 South Wells Street, Chicago, 1984–86, by Bertrand Goldberg Associates Inc, is a five-phase 1.6 km (1 mile) long development site on the bank of the south branch of the Chicago River. The overall megastructure consists of two parallel s-shaped residential blocks, connected by a glazed atrium that rests on a rectilinear four-storey commercial base. The stunning circular geometry was achieved by using a series of vertical concrete tubes, spaced at intervals along the bending perimeter of two adjoining half-circles. Single columns have been placed at the half-way mark to support the floor slabs. There are 22 varieties of apartments divided between 446 units. The glass-covered ten-storey atrium forms a kinetic internal street*

Unconventional multi-unit housing blocks

The Byker Wall Housing Scheme, Newcastle, England, 1969–75, by Ralph Erskine (*below*), which sports a shed roof to suggest domesticity and to protect against rain; brightly coloured, sprawling balconies to add a human touch and variety; interwoven bricks of different colours to break down the mass, and delicate entrance structures to ensure a gradual transition from public to private worlds. The future inhabitants were consulted about their wishes by Erskine, a member of Team X

Gallaratese Apartment Block, Milan, 1969–73, by Aldo Rossi (*illustrated facing page top left*). It has a repetitive simple linearity and a monotonous street gallery that runs the entire length of the four-storey building. It brings together the imagery of a viaduct, the traditional Italian arcades and the organisation of Le Corbusier's *Unités d'habitation*

Noisy-le-Grand housing, Marne-la-Vallée, France, 1978–83, by Henri Ciriani; an elongated bar raised on piers which was another descendant of Le Corbusier's *Unités d'habitation*

Quinta da Malagueira, near Evora, Portugal, begun in 1977 by Alvaro Siza; the rebuilding of an entire quarter that lay between the old town and the countryside, where a low-rise, high-density pattern transformed the traditional patios and street plan from the Portuguese tradition to suit changing social needs. The architect used whitewashed cubic forms, interspersed with terraces and voids filled with deep shadow, to fit in with the landscape

The stylistic and ideological ideas that followed ranged beyond postmodernism alone, for they included also a great number of mature works of a high order which stood outside the ephemeral changes of mere fashion. The debate concerning the relative merits of modernism and postmodernism to some extent continued to cloud the 1980s, but hindsight suggests that postmodernism was a short-lived excursion and a relatively local phenomenon. Until the remarkable developments of technology and engineering during the late twentieth century, architecture around the world had developed a relatively basic vocabulary of forms and structures, possibly because of the limited range of durable construction materials. True innovation inevitably was quite rare, although fresh ways of using this vocabulary have evolved from time to time, and generally the aim was to refine existing capabilities. In spite of contemporary commentators' competing claims that the refiners and the innovators were bringing about major changes, real architectural achievement in the last quarter of the past century has had more to do with evolution and reassessment than revolution and breakthroughs.

The 1980s also witnessed the onset of a postindustrial revolution that was based on electronic handling of information. This meant that towns, homes and offices alike have required hugely increased provision for cabling, and that in time not only has the distinction between home and office become increasingly blurred for many workers, but also that new kinds of work such as call centres, which are based on information technology, have set new challenges.

This technological revolution has forged a new urban model, in both the developing countries and the developed nations, and been the driving force supporting the globalisation of commerce. Local traditions and indigenous crafts are less used in vernacular architecture, leading to a loss of regional identity, as multi-unit housing designs are replicated without any significant changes, using standardized materials.

Throughout the twentieth century the struggle continued to reconcile modernity with tradition. During the postwar years in Germany and Italy and the post-Franco period in Spain, the rigid and bombastic use of the established classical forms in buildings of overpowering scale of the earlier dictatorial regimes resulted in a desire for lighter, more flexible styles of architecture, but traditional forms themselves were reassuring because they were familiar. Attempts to return more directly to this tradition were usually enmeshed with cultural and political overtones. In Britain, this revival of the 1980s was associated with a wave of neo-conservative values in society generally. One example of this assumed good taste and sought-after traditional values that employed neo-Georgian grammar and ornament was the Richmond Riverside development, London, 1985–87, by Quinlan

Terry. Their use was superficial, however, as they lacked the underlying order and measure of the great classical works of antique times on which Georgian building was based.

Such architects, who could be classed as postmodern classicists, were soon criticized for the supposed superficiality of their approach, although they could be almost whimsical in their apparently arbitrary re-use of classical elements. Typical of such buildings was the Marne-la-Vallée housing, Paris, 1978–83, by Richard Bofill, in which giant precast concrete and glass columns were improbably attached to the curving façade of an apartment building.

Aldo Rossi's Gallaratese apartment block in Milan, *illustrated above*, had subtle allusions to pediments; the formally-grouped structural elements recalled rows of columns. In Germany, the Frankfurt Architecture Museum, 1983, by Oswald Mathias Ungers, was a neo-rationalist structure that is based on the theme of buildings within buildings, and alludes to basic forms such as the temple, the aedicule or canopied niche, and the hut.

Berlin staged the *Internationale Bauausstellung* (IBA) exhibition in 1987. The programme that it illustrated was probably the most important and ambitious architectural scheme of recent times. Its primary aim was that of urban repair in a city that was still in

Above: *the entrance to the Victoria apartment block, a* Neubau *construction off the Lindenstraße, by Kollhoff & Ovaska. This was one of the largest in southern Friedrichstadt* Below: Altbau *housing block, Luisenstadt, by Wilhelm Holzbauer. He added a new block to existing housing, giving the site a triangular perimeter that has a green courtyard within*

Above: *Hundertwasserhaus, 3 Kegelgasse/Löwengasse, Vienna, 1983–85 by Friedensreich Hundertwasser (1928–2000). This painter trained for only three months as an architect at the Akademie der Bildende Kunst in Vienna in 1948, but became hugely influential in Vienna and elsewhere through his collaboration with architects, particularly on social housing projects in that city*

disarray following the devastation of the Second World War. The IBA Committee had been set up as a planning organisation in 1979. It was given no powers to develop, and its two directors had clearly-defined areas of responsibility. The *Neubau* division was charged with new building and its emphasis was on recreating the grand plan of the baroque extension of the original city centre, providing an environment suitable for contemporary life in the areas destroyed by the war. The *Altbau* dealt with rehabilitation, working in areas which had been extensively damaged but were still occupied by vigorous but deprived communities. Thus both divisions were having to work within the context of history and the problems of the present.

This momentous attempt to produce some 9,000 new or renewed dwellings in the first five years was taking place against a backdrop of debate between the postmodernists and the users of classical elements. The unrealistic target was soon reassessed, and new one agreed, of 3,000 new and 3,000 rehabilitated dwellings by 1987, the 750th anniversary of the founding of the city.

Unfortunately, trying to reinvent a city that relates to the existing fabric and social patterns is much more difficult and time-consuming than either total destruction and redevelopment or building on greenfield sites. The IBA housing, to which both Rossi and Ungers contributed, fell short of its aim of a new urbanism that integrated traditional forms such as the street, façade, stressed entrance and window in a modern environment. Other traditional features such as the historical grid and courtyard pattern were more successfully employed.

However, given the innate limitations of the brief coupled with problems of urgency, with the bureaucracy and the funding organisation, IBA's building achievement has been heroic. In the Netherlands the inner city areas had already been dealt with, and now there was the problem of overcrowding, as postwar baby boomers raising families demanded yet more subsidised housing.

Carel Weeber was awarded more commissions for these district housing schemes than any other. They were based on the edicts of simple construction and traditional solutions of street and urban block. The large overspill development of the Venserpolder, south-east of Amsterdam, comprises boulevards and monotonous city blocks, four or five storeys high. Another of his commissions, the Paperclip housing in Rotterdam, suffers from an inefficient layout and incorporates plastic materials that have not worn well.

Many architects in Europe were constrained by producing work for public servants who were charged with the commissioning of building projects, whose priority was the urgency to supply housing at a price with the fundamentals of good design being only a secondary consideration. Given sufficient freedom, the individual architects often displayed a far deeper insight into the problems of the social functioning of their

buildings. The design of mass housing has a number of applications, and some of the more interesting successes came from architects committed to the problem of designing housing prototypes to deal with such mass urbanisation.

The housing for the Asian Games, New Delhi, by Raj Rewal, was designed as an aggregation of courts, precincts and terraces with separating gates and layers of transition from public to private space. He used standardized units of several types, combined in ways which created variety of both form and aspect. The housing shows the architect's interest in the spatial and social structure of cities in which houses, terraces, streets and courts are locked together in a single system based upon variations of a limited number of structural elements. Furthermore, Rewal did not satisfy himself with a superficially picturesque township; he controlled it with structures that have concrete frames, infilled with brick, and are covered by whitewashed terrazzo finishes of rough grit that is both durable and sensitive to light. The textured amber-coloured surfaces are incised with grooves to emphasise the structural tradition of honey-coloured sandstone panels.

This housing for the Asian Games had demonstrated that a new permanent community could be established in mass housing designed initially as a working showcase. The organisers of the Barcelona Olympics of 1992 developed the idea of building hostel

Above: *Paperclip housing, Rotterdam, 1982, by Carel Weeber, faced with coloured tiles on concrete panels;* below, *a typical unit plan*

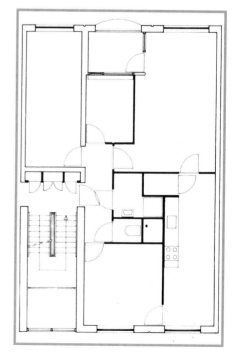

Right: *housing for the Asian Games, New Delhi, 1980–82, by Raj Rewal*

Right: *Villa Olimpica housing, Barcelona, 1989–92, by Carlos Ferrater. The first Olympic village for competitors was built in Los Angeles for the 1932 Games, while more recently the Village in Sydney for the 2000 Olympics opened on 2 September 2000. It immediately became the fifth largest town in New South Wales, Australia, and is not just a dormitory suburb, as the village boasts all of the amenities that a normal town would enjoy*

units, that could be converted to varied family lifestyles, within a far more circumscribed site along the coastal strip.

Among the most successful of the housing schemes raised in the Villa Olimpica were three courtyard blocks by Carlos Ferrater. They were designed to the pre-existing Cerdá grid, and in a Mediterranean courtyard style. They were built on *pilotis* and made varied use in the interiors of the stepped section. Their façades are taut, with angled planes and sharp maritime details in white brick, wood and stainless steel.

Another variation on the theme of mass habitation, which is covered more fully in the next chapter and has become increasingly prominent in recent years, is university campus housing. The student accommodation complex at the Jules Verne High School, Cergy-le-Haut, Cergy Pontoise, north of Paris. made extensive use of steel. Designed by the Architecture Studio and opened in 1993, it forms an integral part of a highly evocative, fascinating and complex mini-city that buzzes with life.

Left: *the student accommodation at Jules Verne High School, Cergy-le-Haut, Cergy-Pontoise, Paris, 1993, by the Architecture Studio*

Chapter Three

Education and Research

THERE WAS A HUGE LEGACY of buildings for educational purposes in Europe from the Victorian era, which were solid and did not need replacement but which were often unsuitable for modern needs. Europe had little by way of a consciously thought-out integrated building programme for education before the First World War, and as on many other aspects of design, its effect was to act as a catalyst for much new thinking. Unfortunately, postwar Europe was short of funds to enact a rebuilding programme that would be sufficient to provide the best learning environment. Educational funding in most countries now comes from a variety of sources, ranging from local, governmental and religious authorities, to private enterprise, across the entire spectrum of education from playgroup to research institute.

Outside the war zone, in north America, ironically the combination of rapid commercialisation with a population explosion had sparked a demand for both new and larger schools and universities. Such pressure, immediately postwar, did not result in any clearly-defined architectural direction but since then there have been considerable advances in the design of educational establishments at all levels.

The period before the First World War was still concerned with *art nouveau*, its various manifestations and a pre-modern style, and while the immediate postwar period saw no clear architectural direction, by the end of the 1920s a number of important and influential educational buildings had been constructed.

In Europe it was initially architects of the modern movement such as Willem Marinus Dudok and Johannes Duiker, working in the Dutch cities of Hilversum and Amsterdam respectively, who began building the new schools. The modern movement made its mark on education in Germany also, and no building was more influential than Gropius' Bauhaus complex.

The Bauhaus buildings were completed in 1926 at Dassau, following the school's move from Weimar. The main block, which

Facing page: the main visitor entrance to the British Library, St Pancras, London, 1962–97, by Colin St John Wilson, eventually opened after a wait of 36 years

Above: *the Bauhaus building, Dessau, 1925–26, by Walter Gropius*
Below: *the west side entrance to the Fagus shoe-last factory, Alfeld, 1911–13, by Walter Gropius with Adolf Meyer and Eduard Werner, was an extension added immediately after the completion of the first new buildings in 1912*

became an icon of the creative early stages of the modern international style, had curtain glass walling, which had first been used by Gropius in the Fagus shoe-last factory, Alfeld, 1911–13. Here it was further refined to show an elegant maturity that symbolized a coming of age of the modern style.

These buildings expressed a clear architectural philosophy. Together with the educational principles and practice that the Bauhaus developed, this was quickly disseminated by former Bauhaus members when they emigrated to settle in other European countries and in north America. For instance, when Gropius arrived in England and entered into partnership with Maxwell Fry, they were responsible for Impington Village College, Cambridgeshire, 1936, the most highly-regarded of new school buildings in the UK of the period.

In the main, however, interwar educational buildings had been essentially utilitarian structures with period embellishments added to indicate their authoritarian character. Impington's simple, functional layout became the model for many more British education authorities after the Second World War, establishing the international style, and probably for the first time the educational needs of the students, as the accepted basis for modern school buildings.

In the immediate postwar years the international style had taken firm roots in America, growing to become the all-consuming passion of virtually all of the creative architects during the next decade. This architectural revolution was inspired by the two Institute of Technology teaching centres at Cambridge, Massachusetts (MIT) and Chicago, Illinois (IIT), the latter being under the direction of Mies van der Rohe who was responsible for the planning of the campus layout between 1940 and 1952. Mies van der Rohe remained at IIT for some 20 years, and designed many of the faculty buildings during his time there. From the unique position that he held, he became the leader by example of early postwar American architecture. The buildings at IIT that he completed confirmed his reputation, such as the Crown Hall which houses the School of Architecture and Design, 1952–56, making him the most influential single figure in American postwar architecture.

Of the buildings at MIT, the meandering Baker House dormitory, 1947–49, was designed by Alvar Aalto in brick with a reinforced concrete frame. It provides accommodation on six floors for a total of 400 students.

These buildings made a considerable impression on Europe because of their evident development and evolution of thought. The postwar baby boom increased the need for school buildings in the UK, and the onset of the 1960s saw an enormously increased provision for higher education.

Mies van der Rohe had an early influence in England, on

the design of the honest steel and brick construction of Hunstanton Secondary Modern School, 1954, by Alison and Peter Smithson. The Miesian character is equally evident in the Netherlands, in the glass wall structure of the Academy of Industrial Design and Applied Art, Amsterdam, 1956–58, by Gerrit Thomas Rietveld.

A new form of expressionist architecture, which attempted to convey something of the sensations of the activities that the buildings housed, was being introduced in America by architects such as Eero Saarinan in the 1960s. Yet another thesis, that art is the essence of architecture, and that if the architect creates art, it will be architecture, was being championed by the increasingly influential Louis I Kahn.

Kahn's first major building had been the Yale University Art Gallery, 1951–53, a design that broke away from the prevailing international style. It brought a thoughtful simplicity and directness to an impressive and original design which included a spaceframe ceiling. The spaceframe is a three-dimensional truss framework for enclosing spaces, and is able to resist loads that are applied from any direction. Systems can be designed to cover very large spaces, uninterrupted by support from the ground.

Kahn's style reached maturity between 1957 and 1961, and the first full statement of his philosophy was displayed in the Richards Medical Research and Biology Building, University of Pennyslvania, 1958–60. Here, the service ducts are grouped together in numerous square towers that rise above the outer walls to create a dramatic effect that was akin to brutalism. In his later laboratory building for the Jonas Salk Institute of Biological Studies, La Jolla, California, 1959–65, he used a similar technique, but utilising the space between the storeys on the horizontal plane, rather than towers in the vertical. The building is constructed of reinforced concrete frames and panels, comprising two parallel blocks with a courtyard between them.

This form of construction was influential on the Law and Education Tower, Boston University, 1960–67, by José Luis Sert, although this is a single tower. It stands beside the Charles River, opposite the Married Students' Quarters.

By this time the international style was long past its prime, even though this style had been economically attractive in terms of constructional methods, because it provided accommodation facilities quickly and efficiently; the simpler the form, the more economical it was to build. Thus, because speed and cost had been of the utmost importance, the new structures of the early postwar era had been highly conformist.

Eero Saarinan had designed the Kresge Auditorium at MIT, 1950–55; this revolutionary building has a warped roof on three supports and incorporates a chapel that has undulating inner brick walls and a central opening in a sculptural dome. It provided

Above: *the Baker House student dormitory, Massachusetts Institute of Technology, Cambridge, Massachusetts, 1947–48, by Alvar Aalto*

Below: *part of the project model for the Jonas Salk Institute for Biological Sciences, La Jolla, San Diego, California, 1959–65, by Louis I Kahn*

an inspiration for younger designers. Scarborough College, University of Toronto, 1966, was designed by John Andrews, one of Sert's students at Harvard. This single-building complex designed to accommodate 5000 people follows the escarpment on which it is built, providing all of the necessary college functions within it and linking them by a continuous undercover street.

By contrast in Europe, where little had been built in the way of university and technical college new buildings or extensions, any restrictions that the international style imposed were more easily shrugged off. The realisation grew that great changes would be needed to accommodate educational needs which demanded new forms and buildings, and in the 1960s these were energetically put into practice. Although this did not lead to the creation of a markedly different style, it did encourage more experimentation, particularly in the technological aspects of building.

The list of educational complexes in Europe of the 1960s therefore includes those which were to become the forerunners of a new generation of buildings, particularly those of Dutch architect Aldo van Eyck, who was also a member of Team X. He designed not only schools and orphanages, but also some 650 playgrounds, which he approached with a very humanistic attitude.

Above: *the main block of the Faculty of Engineering, Leicester University, 1962–64, by James Stirling, and,* below, *the exterior of his History Faculty Library, Cambridge, 1964–68*

Denys Lasdun managed successfully to provide a variety of forms, integrating the residential with the educational, in a deftly stratified arrangement of the buildings of the University of East Anglia (UEA), near Norwich, 1962–69. James Stirling's Faculty of Engineering, Leicester University, 1962–64, with James Gowan, is an original and visually-stimulating design, housing students, teaching workshops, research laboratories and lecture halls within a single edifice. It was a benchmark model for the design of new educational buildings, including Stirling's own History Faculty Library building, Cambridge, 1964–68. This was designed in an L-shape, with the arms housing study rooms and offices, and the tower an angled, fan-shaped reading-room that rises to the top of the building from the second floor.

Postmodernism gained its British emancipation in the 1970s with the emergence of the machine-manufactured building, such as Stirling's Olivetti Training School, Haselmere, Surrey, 1969–72. Its character and form were singularly appropriate for the young company executives for whom it was designed, with moulded glass-fibre-reinforced plastic providing the original flowing shape of the building itself.

Other architects in this field included Denys Lasdun at London University, where he redeveloped the School of Oriental and African Studies and the Institutes of Education and Advanced Legal Studies, completed 1973, in a markedly heavier, more solid modern style than that of his UEA ziggurats. At the Gund Hall Graduate School of Design, Harvard University, 1968–72, John Andrews used staggered and glazed exposed-steel trussed roofs over open studio terraces to provide an ambience of greater interaction between the students. Philip Johnson regarded this as one of the six greatest buildings of the twentieth century.

Newer architects designing educational establishments in Italy included Mario Botta, who designed The Middle School, Morbio Inferiore, 1972–77, with three separate wings. The north wing had seven linked classroom blocks with the second wing, the gymnasium and recreational areas, set at an angle to the classrooms. The third wing, comprising the administration and staff rooms, was set at an angle of thirty degrees to the gymnasium wing. Aldo Rossi displayed his rationalist approach in an elementary school at Fagnano Olona, 1974–77, where a circular library was the central focal point.

With the advent of postmodernism in America, the work of other architects such as Robert Venturi and Frank O Gehry added a quality of freshness that brightened the campus scene. The serious purpose behind many of the design solutions was entirely appropriate to the business of education, but their new liveliness, probably highly stimulating to the fertile young minds that were to occupy these buildings, was frequently dismissed as postmodern brashness. This postmodern effect, and the break from normal conventions, can be seen in the fractured geometry and resemblances to abstract sculpture at Gehry's Ignatius Loyola Law School, Los Angeles, 1986, and the Gordon Wu Hall, Butler College, Princeton University, New Jersey, 1983, by Venturi.

Some of the larger projects and the most exciting new buildings were outside the university campus. In Paris the *Bibliothèque national de France* by Dominique Perrault, the largest and the most spectacular library project anywhere in the world, opened in 1996. Its four 100-metre (328ft) high towers in the shape of open volumes are sited around an open sunken garden. Internally the 360,000m² (3,875,000 sq ft) library buildings contain 450 km (280 miles) of bookshelves and in the lecture rooms there are 4,000 seats. The *Bibliothèque* had taken eight years

Below: *the façade of Gordon Wu Hall, Butler College, Princeton University, New Jersey, 1983, by Robert Venturi*

Right: *the four 'open book' towers of the* Bibliothèque Nationale de France, *Paris, 1988–96, by Dominique Perrault*

to construct, and during that time there was much modification.

Similarly in London, the new British Library eventually opened at St Pancras, London, in 1997, a year after its French counterpart. The plans for the work by Colin St John Wilson had first been unveiled in 1962; the 36 years of debate and building cost an estimated £500 million.

Costing a little less at $1,050 per m² (£65 per sq ft), and not taking nearly so long, was the Central Library, Phoenix, Arizona, 1988–95, by Will Bruder. The library, constructed around a five-storey central atrium, has an area of 26,000 m² (280,000 sq ft), a glass-covered southern elevation and used 40,000 kg (40 tons) of ribbed copper cladding on its exterior area. Its five floors include audio and video libraries in addition to the traditional book library, a childrens' reading room, a theatre and a café.

A plethora of smaller individualised buildings in education were completed during the early 1990s, including

• Biological Science Facility, University of Washington, Seattle, by Studio TRA. This practice also designed the Kotzebue Technical Center, Alaska, and a primary school at Dillingham, Alaska, both of which called for a vastly different approach, mostly aimed at the students' comfort and well-being in the harsh climate, rather than the buildings' external physical appearances.

Three new American libraries: above, *the main public library, San Francisco, 1996, by James Ingo Freed of Pei Cob Freed and Partners;* right, *the Central Library, Phoenix, Arizona, 1988–95, by Will Bruder; and* far right, *the Harold Washington Library, Chicago, 1991–93, by Hammond, Beeby & Babka*

- S Giorgetto School complex, Anagni, near Rome, by Massimiliano Fuksas and Anna Maria Sacconi, in which a primary and a secondary school are combined to include 50 classrooms, two auditoriums, two gymnasiums, a dining hall and two libraries, a triumph of style over architectural function.
- Technical College, Aoyama, Tokyo, 1988–90, by Makoto Sei Watanabe. This extraordinary building has an exterior that perhaps can best be described as organic mechanical, its forms being reminiscent of an Escher engraving. This art school wears its creations on the outside of the building, where the architect's use of space and form defied all architectural conventions.
- *Cité Scolaire Internationale*, Lyon, France, 1985–87, by Jourda et Perraudin Partenaires; this building is shaped like a giant question mark, the long block combining teaching and administration being curled around a sports centre and recreational areas. The entire complex, covering 29,000m² (312,150sq ft), accommodates a primary school, college, high school and a multi-functional sports centre that is open to the public.
- Washington State Ecology Department, Lacey, 1993, by Keating Mann Jernigan Rottet; a building comprising two L-shaped units that house both the offices and facilities for the collections, and a 785-space car park. The general layout creates a carefully-gauged balance between architecture and nature and makes extensive use of mainly locally-produced wood for the interiors. The materials used for the exteriors are decorative cement, stone and glass.
- Department of Chemistry and Biology, University of California, Los Angeles (UCLA), 1994, by Anshen + Allen Architects. This is an addition to a complex of buildings, constructed as two separate L-shapes linked by a staircase, for the specific purposes of the two specialisms, the structures reflecting the needs of each.
- Department of Public Relations, University Institute of Modern Languages, Milan, 1991–93, by Lorenzo Guiducci e Roberto Guiducci; three interconnecting units of which the central six-storey unit is for teaching staff and communal use, with the laboratories and classrooms to the sides. It is a building in a style subtly balanced between discretion and opulence, with a six-storey galleried atrium winter garden, which is lit by one of three skylights. The galleries here are connected by a transparent escalator system, and outside there are arcaded cloisters sheltering meeting places, bars, a bookshop and conference rooms.

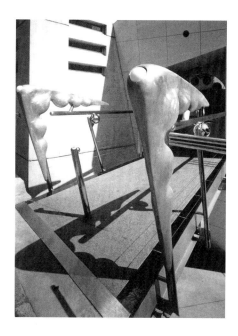

Above: *a walkway with aluminium sculptures over the handrails at the Technical College, Aoyama, Tokyo, 1988–90, by Makoto Sei Watanabe*

Below: *Department of Public Relations, University Institute of Modern Languages, Milan, 1991–93, by Lorenzo Guiducci e Roberto Guiducci*

Chapter Four

Art and Culture

PUBLIC PATRONAGE OF THE ARTS had grown throughout the nineteenth century to play a significant part in cultural life in the wider education of the populace in both Europe and the USA. This provided for the foundation and upkeep of public libraries, museums and art galleries in civic centres by central or local governmental bodies, by raising public subscriptions or by direct private philanthropy. The latter became increasingly important further into the twentieth century, especially among the seriously rich in America, who initiated and supported programmes of building in order to house their collections of art and artefacts which they donated via the trustees of the charitable foundations which they established for the purpose.

It was as a result of this nineteenth-century recognition of the need of both cultural enlightenment and entertainment that such important resources as the Victoria and Albert Museum in London, the Walker Art Gallery in Liverpool, and the John Rylands Library in Manchester were established. For these, the classical style which had dominated throughout the second half of the nineteenth century had produced buildings that reflected civic pride. This idiom therefore predominated at the beginning of the new century until the advent of the modern style. The interwar years provided remarkably few prestigious centres of culture or even individual museums, galleries, theatres, concert halls or libraries; and, given the state of world economies, few were built until after the Second World War. By then, because the buildings themselves were considered to be a reflection of the state of health of a nation's culture, they became important *avant-garde* statements of current taste.

One exception, immediately after the First World War, was Hans Poelzig's *Großes Schauspielhaus*, Berlin, 1919. The theatre was an adaptation of the former covered market of 1865–68 by Friedrich Hitzig, which although providing important benefits of comfort and cleanliness had not been a commercial success, and was used from 1874 for the *Zircus Schumann*. The reconstruction by

Facing page: the Centre National d'Art et de Culture Georges-Pompidou, *Paris, 1977, by Renzo Piano and Richard Rogers, is one of the most excitingly eccentric buildings of the twentieth century*
Below: the Palais de l'Image, *Paris, 1937, by J-C Dondel, A Aubert, P Viard and M Dastuge. It has latterly become the home of several organisations concerned with the preservation of still and moving images. Originally it was the* Palais de Tokyo, *built for the World Fair, and later the* Palais d'Art Moderne, *before the establishment of the* Centre National d'Art et de Culture Georges-Pompidou *and the* Musée d'Orsay, *in the former train station Gare d'Orsay as venues for modern art exhibitions*

Above: *the 5000-seat auditorium of the* Großes Schauspielhaus, *Berlin, 1919, by Hans Poelzig, a remarkable expressionist project*

Poelzig was one of the most heightened examples of expressionist architecture, a loose-knit philosophy of design that had emerged in Germany just before the First World War. In architecture, expressionism followed *art nouveau*, holding that a building should not merely function well, but should evoke sensations. Max Reinhardt, the stage director, was said to have also been involved with the design; the stage projected into the blood-red auditorium specifically for his grandiose productions. The whole treatment was highly dramatic, with stalactite-like acoustical projections descending from the ceiling and an exterior faced with wire-lattice plaster to produce a monumental effect. Sadly, the stalactites were removed in 1938, and the building demolished in 1980.

In the 1920s Rudolf Steiner designed the extraordinary Goetheanum II, Dornach, Switzerland, 1928. This stands on the site of his Goetheanum I (Free High School for Spiritual Science), 1913, a domed timber building that had burned down in 1922. It is still an incredible technical achievement, the world's largest raw concrete structure, built from sectional profile drawings.

Above: *the main entrance façade of* Goetheanum II, *Dornach, near Basel, Switzerland, 1928, by Rudolf Steiner*

Above right: *the Shakespeare Memorial Theatre, Stratford-upon-Avon, Warwickshire, 1929, by Scott, Chesterton & Shepherd. A proposal to demolish the theatre in 2002 aroused much controversy and is still under consideration*

A very different, more prosaic and practical construction appeared in England in 1929. The original Shakespeare Memorial Theatre, Stratford-on-Avon, 1877–79 had been built by public subscription but was destroyed by fire in 1926. Its replacement, by Scott, Chesterton and Shepherd, is constructed in brick and glass and was formally opened in 1932. Since 1961, it has been known as the Royal Shakespeare Theatre.

The first major public commission by Alvar Aalto, won in competition in 1927, was the municipal library, Viipuri, Finland, 1935. This is notable for its functionality, based not only on calculations but on a user-friendly approach, and it remains an important building in the evolution of Finnish architecture.

The Museum of Modern Art, New York, 1939, by Edward Durrell Stone, was the building that introduced the international style to New York. It was extended by Philip Johnson in 1950, but much remains of the original six-storey structure. At the time, America was recovering from the Depression and Europe was concerned with re-arming, so much of the available funds, resources and manpower were diverted to other areas, and for some time building for the arts was forced to take a back-seat role.

New York was also the venue for the superb Solomon R Guggenheim Museum, 1946–59, one of Frank Lloyd Wright's most passionately idiosyncratic and personal expressions. The site was acquired as early as 1947, and initial designs were based on spiral forms dating from before this, but the final design was derided for its supposed vulnerability to fire hazards. The architect defended his vision vigorously; building work began in May, 1957, and the museum opened in a furore of controversy five months after his death in 1959. Today it remains a haven of calm, refreshment and stimulus in the city that never sleeps.

Below left: the South Bank arts centre, London, 1965, by Denys Lasdun

Britain held the Festival of Britain Exhibition in 1951 to celebrate the hundredth anniversary of the Great Exhibition, and the Royal Festival Hall, London, was built to mark the occasion. It was designed by Sir Robert Matthew, the chief architect of the London County Council, and his staff. The building, a concrete box within a concrete box, is architecturally uninspiring, although superb acoustically.

London's south bank complex was extended by the addition of the Queen Elizabeth Hall, 1966, by Hubert Bennett. This seats 1,000, and is also acoustically successful, although externally the exposed shuttered concrete that continued the south bank style has not weathered well and now appears solid, drab and dull.

Above: the Royal Festival Hall, London, 1951, by Sir Robert Matthew is the only building erected for the Festival of Britain Exhibition to remain standing. Its walls are 25.4 cm (10 in) thick, with a cavity of 30.5 cm (12 in) between them

Juan O'Gorman covered the book stack tower of his library for the National Autonomous University of Mexico, 1950–52, in richly decorated mosaics, and the library of St John's University, Collegeville, Minnesota, 1953–61, designed by Marcel Breuer was an example of the architect's undoctrinaire modernism. Alvar Aalto's House of Culture, Helsinki, 1953–58, was sponsored by left-wing union organisations and erected in a working-class area. It included a cinema, concert hall, apartments and offices. The hall had a multi-usage auditorium, faced in wedge-shaped bricks designed by the architect to give a curved surface. Le Corbusier's Youth Centre, Firminy, France, 1956–65, was among his last designs to be built before his death. Sited on sloping ground, the building has a swooping roofline reminiscent of Ronchamp.

It was really in the next decade, the 1960s, that money became available for the building of new centres for the arts, which are as diverse in style or aesthetic form as they are in use. By this time, the use of public money for cultural activities had become a political issue, and in addition to the private patronage of an individual or wealthy family trust, industries or manufacturers began to sponsor museums of their products and commissioned appropriate buildings in which to exhibit them.

Hans Scharoun's Philharmonic Hall, Berlin, 1963, reflects the architect's expressionist background, and fuses an expressive understanding of the experience of concertgoing with dramatic structural forms enclosed by a tentlike roof. His Berlin State Library was begun in 1967 but only completed in 1978 and has similarities with the Philharmonic Hall, as the interiors of both buildings are carefully considered and beautifully finished.

The Library of Oita, Japan, 1962–66, by Arata Isozaki, was influenced by Le Corbusier's *béton brut*, and represents the early stages of the postwar modern movement's conquest of Japan.

Right: the Berlin Philharmonic Concert Hall, Berlin, 1956–63, by Hans Scharoun, has an auditorium which was conceived as a multifaceted vessel, with angular forms, tilted planes and stratified trays of seats floating at different levels

Galleries and museums of the 1960s ranged from the decorative neo-classicism of the Huntington Hartford Gallery of Modern Art, New York, 1964, by Edward Durrell Stone, enlivened by Moorish pierced decoration, to the strict application of the international style as at the National Gallery, Berlin, 1967–68, by Mies van der Rohe, influenced by early principles based on classical proportions and mimicking a temple on a podium with a horizontal pediment. The ziggurat-like platform complex of the Oakland Museum, California, 1968, by Kevin Roche and John Dinkeloo, integrates three separate museums into a single reinforced-concrete unit, also encompassing offices, a garage and an auditorium. Alvar Aalto's North Jutland Museum, Alborg, Denmark, 1969–73, is a classic of good museum design with its controlled even light, adequate exhibition space and clear, comprehensive circulation system, with the galleries being arranged around a lecture theatre.

Above: *the Vredenburg Music Centre, Utrecht, the Netherlands, 1979, by Herman Herzberger*

Cultural buildings of the 1970s

1968–78 East Building, National Gallery of Art, Washington DC, by I M Pei; a clear derivation of the international style, it displays an aggressive exterior. Inside, the lighting from the glazed triangular roof throws intrusive shadows over the exhibition area.

1970–74 Art Museum, Takasaki, Japan, by Arata Isozaki; a cube module based on sides 12 m (35 ft 4 in) long, with the rectangular shape of its main body interrupted by a diagonal extension that has an open lower floor.

1972–74 Municipal Art Museum, Kitakyushi, Japan, by Arata Isozaki; two square blocks positioned over the canopied entrance dominate the complex.

1972–75 Miró Museum, Barcelona, by José Luis Sert; a varied and interesting design, with exposed shuttered concrete and curved forms, based on the modern style that shows great sensitivity about the building's use.

1972–82 *Städtisches Museum Abteiberg*, Mönchengladbach, Germany, by Hans Hollein; a metal-clad building like an industrial warehouse, with light admitted via north-facing horizontal windows. Its square individual rooms are accessed via open corners, providing extensive uninterrupted diagonal vistas. The complex also includes a tall administration building of workshops and storage rooms, and a separate pavilion for temporary exhibitions.

1973 extension, Boston Public Library, by Philip Johnson; situated in a side street, it ignores the Italian palazzo design characteristics of the original building. The extension has three large arches and no cornice.

1973–75 Central Library, Kitakyushi, Japan, by Arata Isozaki; an international style building, with echoes of Le Corbusier's Ronchamp chapel in its dark dome shapes above concrete walls.

1975–79 the Atheneum, New Harmony, Indiana, by Richard Meier; this small cultural centre set in open parkland is a complex of curved and rectilinear solids and calculated voids.

1977 *Centre National d'Art et de Culture Georges-Pompidou*, Paris, by Renzo Piano and Richard Rogers; designed when these architects were relatively unknown, on completion it became one of the most talked-about buildings in the world. It grew to become enormously influential, giving a new authority to this high-tech approach to modern architectural form and structure, which reveals how the building works. The Pompidou Centre became its first monument, revealing the extent to which building relies on engineering technology, and demonstrating that the skeleton is as interesting and as beautiful as the skin beneath which it normally lies.

1977–84 *Neue Staatsgalerie* extension, Stuttgart, by James Stirling with Michael Wilford; a most impressive complex, drawing together elements of high tech with postmodernism and displaying much inventiveness. This is combined internally with a sensitive provision of space, and a great variety in circulation pattern. Most of the postmodernist elements are drawn from classical sources, often taking the form of elaborate jokes.

1978 Sainsbury Arts Centre, University of East Anglia, Norwich, by Norman Foster; this much-criticised isolated building has a classically-proportioned, rectangular form of metal-truss construction and metal sheet cladding. Rounded corners soften the edges while the clear internal space provides for a variety of uses.

1979 Vredenburg music centre, Utrecht, by Herman Herzberger; a central auditorium surrounded by a thriving complex of shops, restaurants, and pedestrian walkways that connect it to the new city centre, and extensive bicycle parking space.

1979 Floating Theatre, Venice, by Aldo Rossi; constructed from a timber frame and battening, this small theatre on a barge on the Grand Canal takes its form from medieval and Renaissance inspirations, echoing the past glories of Venetian pageantry.

1979–84 Fogg Museum, Harvard University, Cambridge, Massachussetts, by James Stirling; a building that shows postmodernist characteristics, it is essentially similar to this architect's contemporaneous *Neue Staatsgalerie* extension, Stuttgart, 1977–84.

1979–84 *Museum für Kunsthandwerk*, Frankfurt, Germany, by Richard Meier; a new complex which incorporates the old home of the museum. It is significant that the interiors of the three new building volumes which now house the collection of arts and crafts were planned by the architect's office on the basis of detailed lists of the exhibits.

The landmark Opera House by Jørn Utzon and others was under construction on a tongue of land in Sydney Harbour between 1957–70. Its form, that was intended to echo sailing boats dotting the harbour, took precedence over the needs of opera, lighting, acoustics or even the shape of the site on which it stood. Following many protests and even debates in Parliament, the architect resigned. The revised design provided two adjacent auditoria with shell vaults, spherical segments locked together, more like a cluster of molluscs.

The auction room for the abbatoir at La Villette, Paris, originally constructed in 1969, was closed at the same time as the slaughterhouse in 1974, and converted into the *Cité des Sciences et de l'Industrie*, at the Parc de la Villette, which also includes the *Grande Halle*, the *Zénith*, and the later *Cité de la Musique*. This massive space of 270 m (885 ft) x 110 m (360 ft) x 49 m (160 ft) high occupies a volume three times that of the original *Centre National d'Art et de Culture Georges-Pompidou*, achieved by removing all internal partitions, and the whole project was led by Adrien Fainsilber.

This architect designed the *Géode*, a spherical polished stainless-steel structure poised above an expanse of water between the museum and its park, thus both reflecting its surroundings and reflected in them. The internal tree-structure is independent, supporting the tiers of seats for this hemispherical cinema, where the viewer sits in the centre of the image.

A number of major commissions during the 1970s were postmodern in treatment, following the classically-inspired small-scale buildings of the previous decade. At the same time high-tech was becoming fashionable, and both styles continued to be extensively exploited into the 1980s as the leading architects exhibited an increasing internationalism.

Above: *the Sydney Opera House, 1957–70, by Jørn Utzon*

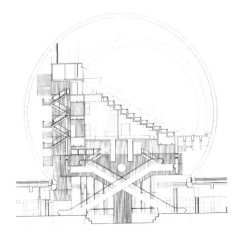

Above: *north-south section of the* Géode, Cité des Sciences et de l'Industrie, *La Villette, Paris, 1980–85, by Adrien Fainsilber*

Right: *the* Géode *is a compact ball with no apparent entrance and a reflective skin of 6,433 small triangles covered by polished stainless steel. Inside there is a cinema with 357 seats set out in tiers at a 30-degree slope to the 1,000m² (10,764sq ft) screen*

Similarly, the increased leisure time in which to pursue individual interests stimulated a growing attraction to the arts and a widening of horizons in the general public as populations in the developed world enjoyed a period of exponential economic growth. There was a corresponding wave of construction across Europe, Japan and the United States to satisfy the growing appetite for cultural leisure activities. This new wealth of towns and cities transformed their museums into the new cathedrals, as culture replaced religion as the central significance in many more lives. Increased aesthetic appreciation of in the population generally coincided with a more symbiotic relationship between architects and the uses to which their creations were put, and this improved co-operation began to yield more individualistic buildings towards the end of the 1980s.

In France, and particularly in Paris, François Mitterrand instigated a series of cultural projects, the *Grands Travaux*. These included the redesign of the Louvre Museum, including the redevelopment of the Richelieu Wing, which gave the Museum a new entrance located in the centre of the structure, in an area which until then had been used as a car park. This entrance, which was opened in 1989, was the now-famous pyramid designed by I M Pei. The Richelieu Wing was completed in 1993.

The success of the Louvre pyramid prompted other French cities to embark on equally ambitious projects. At Nîmes, on a site previously occupied by an opera house of 1803 and facing the *Maison Carrée* Roman temple, *c* 12BC, the *Carré d'Art* public library and *Médiathèque* art museum complex, 1985–93, by Norman Foster, represents a classical solution to the introduction of a subtle high-tech building into a historic urban environment.

Meanwhile, elsewhere in Europe new museums varied between the *Museum Moderner Kunst*, Frankfurt, 1982–90, by Hans Hollein, and Frank O Gehry's rather small Vitra Museum, Weil-am-Rhine, Germany, 1986–89. Designed to display the company's furniture, the latter is not only an exciting and unusual kaleidescope of soaring spaces; also it was a forerunner to the architect's sensational Guggenheim Museum, Bilbao, 1991–97. Another notable achievement was the unusually-sited Groninger Museum, Groningen, the Netherlands, 1990–94, by Alessandro Mendini and others.

There was little governmental funding of national museums in Japan, so in the closing years of the twentieth century, local government, private companies and individuals made Japan one of the most active countries in creating new museums. This cultural building programme, headed by the architect Arata Isozaki, was continued in such works as the National Museum of Modern Art, Kyoto, 1983–86, by Fumihiko Maki; the Yatsushiro Municipal Museum, Kumamoto, 1989–91, by Toyo Ito, and the Naoshima Museum and hotel, Kagawa, 1990–92, by Tadao Ando.

Cultural buildings begun in the early 1980s

1980–83 Civic Centre, Tsukuba, Japan, by Arata Isozaki; in a new town which is a centre for scientific and technological research, the building is an intriguing mixture of eastern and western symbolism. Its piazza is bounded on two sides by a range of different-scale buildings and has a sunken oval centre, in the middle of which is an opening into which a stream drains. In general, the Centre has postmodern classical derivations combined with metallic high-tech and traditional garden arrangements.

1980–86 National Museum of Roman Art, Mérida, Spain, by José Rafael Moneo; a unique brick building lit by glazed bands in the ceiling of a tall central nave and overhead windows in side walls above a row of small niches.

1981–86 Museum of Contemporary Art, Bunker Hill, Los Angeles, California, by Arata Isozaki; his first American work, clad in red sandstone over a red granite base, complemented by dark-green painted aluminium panels with pink diagonal jointing.

1981–86 De Menil Collection, Houston, Texas, by Renzo Piano; sited in a small park. The traditional timbered walls and verandahs of the surrounding suburban housing were replicated in Piano's design. The building houses Dominique de Menil's art collection, in addition to being a centre for music, literature, the theatre, cultural and educational activities. The structure is both flexible and open, lit by natural light, with a roof of ferro-concrete leaves.

1982–84 Okanoyama Graphic Art Museum, Nishiwaki, Hyogo, Japan, by Arata Isozaki; inspired by the nearby railway line, its rooms are linked together like carriages, and are used to exhibit, in a chronological succession, the works of the artist Tadanori Yokoo.

1983 Regional Library, San Juan Capistrano, California, by Michael Graves; typical of his attachment to postmodernism, but more subdued than many of his other large projects.

1983 High Museum of Art, Atlanta, Georgia, by Richard Meier; fashionable version of the international style with postmodern connections, following to a large degree his Frankfurt *Museum für Kunsthandwerk*. It is based on three cubes occupying the corners of a square, and there is a long diagonal ramp linking the entrance to the road. The Museum contains galleries on six floors with panoramic internal vistas and is faced in white porcelain-enamel panels, giving it a clinical external appearance.

Above: *the entrance to the Kunstforum, Vienna, 1988–92, by Gustav Peichl, evokes memories of the Sezession*

Below: *the American Heritage Center, Laramie, Wyoming, 1987–93, by Antoine Predock*

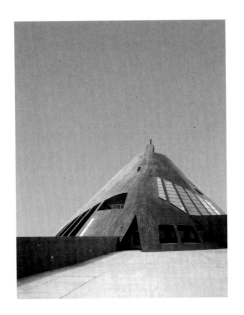

In America there is also virtually no central government support, but instead a culture of financial encouragement for individual donations. The boom in the creation of new museums of the early 1980s slowed down considerably towards the end of the decade, but the 1990s still provided the country with some outstanding and diverse structures, including:

- American Heritage Center, Laramie, Wyoming, 1987–93, by Antoine Predock; an unusually-shaped building which recalls the nearby mountains, and which has been described as geologically-oriented modernity. Situated in a 10 ha (24.71 acre) site, at the centre of the building is a tepee-like patinated copper cone which houses a research facility for students. The long main building forms a terraced volume with a flat roof and houses the University of Wyoming Art Museum. The concrete blocks from which it was built were specially formed with a coarse aggregate and sandblasted in order to imitate the finish of original adobe constructions.

- Museum of Modern Art, San Francisco, California, 1990–94, by Mario Botta; this massive building, clad in a brick veneer, claims for itself an important air by its size and differentiation from its surroundings. A flamboyant central feature is a typical Botta truncated cone, in this instance an oculus which provides light via its glazed roof through the five storeys. The Museum was part of an urban redevelopment programme, covering more than 40 ha (99 acres) and its funding, said to amount to some $60m (£40m), was provided almost entirely from private donations.

- Rock and Roll Hall of Fame, North Coast Harbor, Cleveland, Ohio, 1993–95, by I M Pei; a controversial tribute to the idea of architecture as 'frozen music', sited on the shores of Lake Erie. Pei designed a 50 m (164 ft) concrete tower which helps to support a 35 m (115 ft) high triangular glass tent housing the spectacular entrance lobby, closely related to his Louvre pyramid. Beneath the tent is a public plaza, and below that some 3,000 m² (32,292 sq ft) of exhibition space. A theatre is contained in a cantilevered trapezoid form poised over the lake, and a balancing cantilevered drum houses a dance arena. A café overlooking the entrance space is on the third floor of the tower, with the hall of fame itself at the top. It is the centrepiece of a $300m (£200m) development, known as North Coast Harbor.

The *Cité de la Musique*, Parc de la Villette, Paris, 1990, by Christian de Portzamparc, won the *l'Equerre d'Argent* prize in 1988, and the *Grand Prix de l'Architecture* in 1990. The complex, a collection of skilfully-designed architectural pieces in symmetrical and asymmetrical compositions of rectangles, trapeziums, and spheres, is like a contemporary city in a state of evolution, full of strange buildings that continually catch the eye. It was designed to host a wide range of musical styles, from jazz to classical, each with its own particular requirements.

The complex is split into two separate sections, divided by a courtyard, the *Place aux Lions*. The section to the west, a building of four units partially fitted with an extended roof, houses the school of music and dance. The eastern section is constructed around the large ellipital concert hall, with the communal areas and internal circulation areas completely glazed and transparent, creating extensive areas of light around the dense, opaque structures of the acoustic shells of the work rooms. This section is home also to the headquarters of the *Ensemble Intercontemporain*, a music museum, smaller concert halls, a centre for the study of musical instruments, teaching institute, an amphitheatre, rehearsal rooms and a shopping area.

In Japan, two outstanding and divergent concert halls completed the century. The Kirishima International Concert Hall, Aira, 1994, by Fumihiko Maki, complex was built on a site of 44,800 m² (482,227 sq ft), with one single, rather elongated, construction, that looks like a beached ship. Designed with a carefully judged understatement, in addition to the leaf-shaped

Above: *the spiral-shaped path leading to the rehearsal rooms and* below, *the east sector of the* Cité de la Musique, *Paris, 1990, by Christian de Portzamparc*

Facing page: *the Joán Miró library, Barcelona, 1982–85, by Beth Galí, Màrius Quintana and Antoni Solanas is situated in a clearing of a pine wood and surrounded by a lake;* below *is the library with the main entrance to the left and* above, *a side ramp which leads to the terrace and upper floor*

Below: *the façade of the three-storey 13,800 m² (148,543 sq ft) Museum of Contemporary Art, Barcelona, 1987–95, by Richard Meier, tinted by the setting sun*

main concert hall with seating for 800, it accommodates rehearsal rooms, offices, dressing rooms, and seminar rooms. The main hall is built to allow a variable stage size, and there is a separate outdoor amphitheatre which seats 4000.

The Symphony Garden, Sakai-minato, Japan, 1994, by Shin Takamatsu, is designed in the form of a large public garden for city-dwellers. The cylindrical structure, a venue for concerts, conferences and theatrical performances, is surrounded by the Flower Ring of reinforced concrete, 10.8 m (35.43 ft) tall and 66 m (216.55 ft) in diameter, leading to the flower garden on the hall roof. The path on this ring is planted with seasonal flowers and acts as a gallery for the open-air theatre, with waterfalls for curtains and an artificial pool of 7000 m² (75,350 sq ft) for the stage, which has underwater lighting. The auditorium seats just 400 and is enclosed by a curved ceiling and walls, intended to provide a uniform quality acoustic.

In 1999, Barcelona became the first-ever city to be awarded the Royal Institute of British Architects' gold medal. Newer buildings meriting the award included *L'Auditori*, an extraordinary minimalist concert hall completed in 1999, by Rafael Moneo. Strictly rectangular in plan, the complex looks inward on itself; the somewhat low-key exterior is severely clad in black oxidised steel, yet in contrast the interiors of the beautifully serene foyer and

main hall are lined in purest white maple wood. In addition to this symphony hall with seating for 2340, there are two chamber halls, a conservatoire, a music museum and all the usual rehearsal rooms and administration offices, arranged around a courtyard under Moneo's 'skylight impluvium'. This is an inversion of the ancient Roman *impluvium*, the square basin at the centre of the atrium of the house, that caught the rainwater from the open space in the roof; Moneo's impluvium allows the light to pour in.

Together with *L'Auditori* by the Plaça de les Glòries is Richard Bofill's magnificent new *Theatre Nacional de Catalunya*, 1997, where the main auditorium seats 900 and has a cross-shaped stage with 40 m (131 ft) space over it to facilitate scene changes. There is an outer curtain wall and an inner one of architectural precast concrete, the single metal gable roof resting on concrete columns. The three-storey Museum of Contemporary Art, 1987–95, by Richard Meier, is considered by the architect as one of his more successful buildings. It has all of the hallmarks of Meier's mature style, with its louvred glazing and white metal and stucco exterior.

The Joan Miró Library was one of the earlier group of cultural buildings to be erected in the city. Begun in 1982, the library was the design of Beth Galí, Màrius Quintana and Antoni Solanas, and was planned to blend with its newly-created park environment, exploiting this natural setting to the full.

Chapter Five

Leisure and Recreation

THE DEVELOPED WORLD witnessed a considerable range of changes in the patterns of leisure and recreational pursuits throughout the twentieth century. Leisure, once the domain of the privileged few in society, became available to all in the West as social and economic conditions improved in the period of recovery after two world wars. As working hours were reduced, wages increased and welfare states provided benefits hitherto undreamed of, particularly in health care and education. People now live longer and are active well into their post-retirement years, and in comparison with the early twentieth century all age groups have an exponentially increased disposable income and more leisure in which to enjoy it.

Sports stadia

Architectural character is closely allied to use; just as cultural and religious structures convey a certain spirituality, so the concept of buildings allied to leisure and recreation should evoke something of the spirit of engagement, excitement, fulfillment and success. The first Olympic Games of the modern era were held in Athens in 1896, a year after the first professional, officially-recognised American football match. The first Davis Cup tennis match took place in 1900, and the modern baseball World Series began in 1903. Therefore, the provision of adequate accommodation for all of these increasingly popular sports was essentially a twentieth-century development.

The first Olympic complex to be built specifically for a full range of events was at White City, London, for the 1908 games. Adolf Hitler decided that the 1936 Games, held in Berlin, should embody the power and authority of the Third Reich, and made elaborate arrangements to achieve this by the provision of magnificent facilities. The Olympic Stadium, Helsinki, was originally designed in the modern style by Yrjö Lindegren for the

Above: *the architecturally ground-breaking Millennium Dome, London, 1999, by Richard Rogers Partnership*
Facing page: *the Gare do Oriente railway station, 1998, by Santiago Calatrava, combines the Lisbon Metro system and a major suburban bus terminus and was built to link the commercial heart of the city with the Expo '98 site*
Below: *Hitler's Olympic showpiece, the Reichsportsfeld, Berlin, 1934–36, by Werner March as improved by Albert Speer*

Above: *the Olympic sports halls, Tokyo, 1961–64, by Kenzo Tange with URTEC*

Above: *the Olympic tent, München, 1968–72, by Behnisch & Partners, Frei Otto, Leonhardt and Andrä*
Right: *the* Palazzetto dello Sport, *Rome, 1956–57, by Pier Luigi Nervi and Annibale Vitellozzi, built to accommodate 5000 spectators for the 1960 Rome Olympics; it was followed by the larger* Palazzo dello Sport, *far right, 1958–60, by Marcello Piacentini, which was crowned by a hemispherical dome supported on diagonal posts and accommodated 16,000 spectators. The circular outer skin was entirely glazed*

Games in 1940, but was modified and clad in timber by Toivo Jäntti for the postponed meeting in 1952. For the 1964 Olympics in Tokyo, Kenzo Tange produced two covered structures combining Japanese character with modern engineering expertise, the Olympic pool being covered by a seductive double-curving elliptical roof that swings around concrete masts.

The then largest non-Olympic indoor swimming pool in the world, the striking Empire Swimming Pool, Wembley, London, 1934, by Sir Owen Williams, was constructed from reinforced concrete with exposed shuttering. The sides were strengthened with concrete fins, and the roof was supported on three hinged arches with a span of more than 72 m (236 ft).

Immediately after the Second World War, the properties of reinforced concrete were further explored, especially by such pioneers as Pier Luigi Nervi. He designed the *Palazzetto dello Sport*, Rome, 1956–57. This has a 50 m (164 ft) diameter dome that is supported by radial buttresses, secured by an underground pre-stressed concrete ring. Other reinforced concrete stadia of the period included the Ingalls Ice Hockey Rink, Yale University, 1958, by Eero Saarinen, a sculptural building which has a roof that swoops across the length of the rink, supporting a cable structure which meets another elliptical curve at the lower roofline.

The selection of the site, integration with transport, the planning and organisation of non-sporting elements such as restaurants and retail space that must be included in order to ensure daily use of a new sports facility by the wider community are all absolutely vital, before construction can begin. Such ancillary facilities greatly enhance the surrounding environment, and make their presence felt on the local cityscape. Recently within the UK these considerations have been lacking, so that the buildings have been perceived as a wasted opportunity rather than a stroke of good fortune for the places where they were built.

Such careful planning and programming resulted in one of the most outstanding of recent architectural successes, the construction of spectacular new sports facilities for the 1992 Olympics in Barcelona. Here the transformation of the city which these brought about breathed new life into it and resulted in the accolade of 1999, when Barcelona became the first-ever city to be awarded the Royal Institute of British Architects' gold medal.

Often the construction of a new sports facility, in enhancing the quality of the cityscape, instigates a change in behavioural patterns, in that it provides a centre for people to meet. This change is perhaps most striking in older suburban areas where new facilities have modernised and enlarged the inner-city fabric.

There may be no finer example of the effect of a new sports stadium on a city than that of the multi-purpose Louisiana Superdome, New Orleans, *illustrated right*. Although primarily an arena for American football, this public assembly facility includes four ballrooms, two restaurants, a clubhouse, numerous meeting rooms and an ample supply of bars and cocktail lounges. This enormous project gave a much-needed lift to what had become a run-down district as the city slipped from having been the largest in the south to only fifth by the time that it was opened, in 1975. It came to represent not only the power and the strength of the athlete, but also a focus for local belief and self-esteem. This aided a recovery that helped to entice a cluster of towering skyscrapers and vast luxury hotels to the central business area of New Orleans, which had grown to become part of a major tourist attraction and centre for business conventions by 1990.

The intelligent approach to urban development for the 1992 Olympics in Barcelona transformed that city and provided others with a shining example of how to mediate between the past and the future. The new and redeveloped sports stadia included the new Sant Jordi Sports Hall for indoor events, *illustrated right*, erected on the hill of Montjuic overlooking the main Olympic stadium and the city. It was designed by Arata Isozaki as a covered stadium, using the Pantadome System. This allowed for the construction of the entire dome on site, where it was built in geometric segments and then raised and folded into position by hydraulic jacks that lifted the structure to its full height of 45 m (148 ft), its metal roofing supported by 62 columns.

Below: *the Palais Omnisports de Bercy, Paris, begun in 1991, by Didier Drummond; it is a sunken open space with tiers of seats cut into the landscape*
Left: *the Ice Rink, Oxford, 1983, by Nicholas Grimshaw*

Notable exotic cinemas

Universum Cinema, Berlin 1926–28,
by Erich Mendelsohn, *illustrated above*,
which was part of a larger, horseshoe-
shaped complex that included a hotel,
restaurant and apartment blocks.
Egyptian Cinema, Essex Road,
London, 1930, by George Coles,
which employed a popular, colourful
Egyptian theme to suggest a tomb of
riches and fantastic dreams.
Grauman's Chinese Theatre,
Los Angeles, 1927, by Meyer and
Holler who employed another
obvious, exotic style.

Broadcasting and cinemas

The first cinema opened in Pittsburgh, Pennsylvania, in 1905, and
with it came the opportunity of another architectural approach to
auditorium design. The screen was raised above the normal stage
level, so that the auditorium floor could be raked from a level
below the stage to a point well above it. Given that human eyes can
accommodate to oblique viewing of the screen and that therefore
frontal viewing is not essential, the fixed relationship between the
location of the projector, the screen and the audience allowed for
a fanned auditorium. Furthermore, acoustics were not a problem
as the sound was recorded and speakers could be positioned all
around. This became of more significance after the introduction of
stereo recording in 1958. Because there was no established
historical form to follow externally, cinema building was
unconfined by precedent and could allow taste or extravagance
full play, to encourage a belief in the celluloid world of fantasy.

During the inter-war years most cities and large towns
acquired purpose-built cinemas, but their size, quality of building,
and the array of outlandish styles used was almost infinite. These
were the golden years of Hollywood, but their uncontested days
had been numbered since 1921, when the first radio broadcast was
made. Even worse was to follow, when the first televison
transmission was made from Alexandra Palace, London, in 1936,
and the cinema became a fast-disappearing building form after the
Second World War until its renaissance as the multiplex during
the last years of the century.

Art Deco coincided with the
golden age of the cinema; above,
the Grandview Theater, St Paul,
displays a typical exterior
Facing page: three British
cinemas with Art Deco interiors;
left centre, the Cavendish
Cinema, Nottingham; left below,
the Savoy Cinema, Hayes,
Middlesex; and right below, the
Odeon Cinema, Camberwell,
London, all of which were
designed by Condecor Ltd

Left: Television Tower, Ostankino,
Moscow, 1967, by D I Burdin,
L I Batalov and N V Nikitin; a
533 m (1750 ft) monument to the
Soviet Union's technology of the
period. The building was seriously
damaged by fire in 2000
Right: the angle of the stem on the
Montjuic Telecommunications
Tower, Barcelona, 1989–92, by
Santiago Calatrava, acts as a
sundial as the sun crosses the
platform at the base of the stairs

Above: *Rusakov Workers' Club, Moscow, 1927–29, by Konstantin Melnikov*

Clubs

Workers' clubs became a feature of soviet life in the 1920s, but although there were very few new purpose-built buildings, these few did include the Zuyev Club, Moscow, 1926–28, by Ilya Golosov. This featured a squat glazed circular staircase tower at one corner, constrained by a heavy angular frame of horizontally-elongated windows. A club building more obviously influenced by the international style is the Rusakov Workers' Club, Moscow, 1927–29, by Konstantin Melnikov, with its white walls and glazed areas. It has a centrally-placed auditorium with seating for 1400, from which smaller halls extend outwards in raised blocks.

After the Second World War there were buildings such as the Millowners' Association Building, Ahmedabad, India, 1951–54, by Le Corbusier. In this typical example of the architect's work, the simple box shape, disguised by the *brise-soleil*, was entered by a ramp. At the Faculty Club, University of California, Santa Barbara, 1968–69, by Charles Moore, the group of disparate buildings includes a dining room, library and guest rooms in addition to the club, which unite in a reference to Spanish colonial style.

The club-crazy Japanese established modern purpose-built social clubs, in a sort-of postmodern style. Two of the best-known are the Ichi-ban-kan and Ni-ban-kan (No 1 Building and No 2 Building), both built in 1970, by Minoru Takeyama. They catered for as many people as possible, and offered a whole range of delights: clubs, bars, kiosks and department stores. The No 1 Building was a black metal tower with glass wings and an inset showing floor-by-floor advertisements of the facilities on offer.

Parks, gardens and zoos

Below: *this mosaic lizard welcomes visitors to Antoni Gaudí's Parc Güell, Barcelona, 1900–14*

Two of the most important parks were built just before the modern period proper, and by two of the most individual of architects: the wonderfully idiosyncratic Parc Güell, Barcelona, 1900–14, by Antoni Gaudí, and the Midway Gardens, Chicago, 1913–14, by Frank Lloyd Wright. Wright's creation, destroyed within a decade, included a restaurant, an outdoor dining area with an entertainment section, and a stage with a canopied orchestral area.

During the inter-war years London Zoo at Regent's Park acquired a new Penguin Pool in 1934, designed by Berthold Lubetkin with Tecton; this was the first expression in London of the true modern movement. In 1964, the same Zoo acquired another important building, an elephant and rhinoceros house, which was designed by Hugh Casson and Neville Conder. Here the effective use of concrete produced a texture that was sympathetic to both the animals and their hides, while the building's solid mass evokes a symbolic impression of strength.

Bridges, stations and airports

One major impact of the Industrial Revolution of the nineteenth century was the need to transport the new flood of manufactured goods, and this meant that better, faster transport systems were essential. The rapid development and growth of railways was itself part of the revolution and throughout Europe and North America, both roads and railways required new bridges to shorten routes and cut journey times. As time elapsed, these bridges became increasingly more ambitious in scale and refined in engineering.

The Swiss engineer, Robert Maillart, was among the first to conduct practical experiments with reinforced concrete, using it to span by curves. He was responsible for the Tavanasa Bridge over the Verder-Rhine river, Switzerland, 1905, the first bridge in which the arch and the roadway are structurally one, using a three-hinged arch to allow for the expansion and contraction. A quarter of a century later, Maillart's designs appeared to float across the Alpine landscape, attenuated in their overall form and stripped of their structural bones. Later still, he experimented with concrete shell construction, which allowed the thinnest of planar surfaces.

Other important bridges that were completed in the years before the Second World War include the George Washington Bridge, New York, 1931, the Sydney Harbour Bridge, 1932, and the Golden Gate Bridge, San Francisco, 1937. After the War, the first modern cable-stayed bridges were built, in which the bridge decks are directly connected to supporting masts by straight cables: in Germany, the Theodor Heuss, or North, Bridge over the River Rhine at Düsseldorf, 1952, by Fritz Leonhardt, and in Sweden, the bridge at Strömsund, 1956, by Franz Dischinger.

More recent European cable-stayed bridges are yet longer and more spectacular: Skarnsundet Bridge, Norway, 1991, constructed by Gleitbau Salzburg, has a central span of 530 m (1739 ft) secured by 208 cables; the *Pont de Normandie*, built across the estuary of the Seine to link Le Havre and Honfleur, 1994, by SETRA, the French road administration design office, has a span of 856 m (2809 ft). However, to date the longest is in Japan, at 890 m (2920 ft), the Honshu-Shikoku bridge authority's third link between the islands, including the Tatara Bridge, 1999.

During the second half of the twentieth century, suspension bridges were constructed across the Mackinac Straits, Michigan, 1957, by David Steinman; the Verrazano Narrows, New York harbour, 1964, by Othmar Ammann; and, also in 1964, Europe's first long-span suspension bridge across the Firth of Forth, Scotland. The double-deck Tsing Ma suspension bridge, Hong Kong, was constructed in 1997, and the second Honshu-Shikoku link included the Akashi Kaikyo Bridge in 1998, spanning 3911 m (12,832 ft) to become the world's longest overall suspension bridge. The Gladesville Bridge, Sydney, was the world's first

Above: *Tavanasa bridge, Switzerland, 1905, by Robert Maillart*

Below: *the twin-deck Seto Ohashi road and rail bridge, Japan, 1978–88, by Honshu-Shikoku bridge authority, forms one section of one link between the islands of Honshu and Shikoku that includes three suspension bridges, two cable-stayed bridges, one truss bridge and five viaducts*

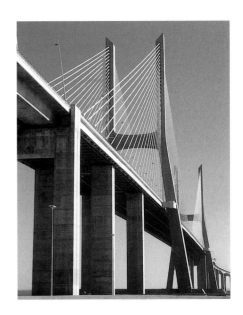

Above left: *Bach de Roda bridge, Barcelona, 1984–87, by Santiago Calatrava, has a steel arch and a compound steel beam structure for the carriageway. He was also responsible for the Campo Volantin footbridge, Bilbao, 1994–97,* above centre, *and the Vasco da Gama bridge, Lisbon, 1998,* above right, *which is 17.7 km (11 miles) long*

Below: *central railway station and airport from* La Città Nuova, *1913–14, by Antonio Sant'Elia*

305 m (1,000 ft) concrete bridge, while the longest concrete arch belongs to the bridge between Krk Island and Croatia, 1980, and the world's longest steel-arch bridge is the New River Gorge Bridge, West Virginia, 1975–78, at 924 m (3030 ft).

Most of the world's great cities had already built Victorian glass and steel rail termini in the railways' heyday, so that for the rest of the twentieth century there was neither a uniform approach, nor a dominant style, evident in architectural development related to transport. Antonio Sant'Elia's futuristic designs for *La Città Nuova*, 1913–14, specified the use of concrete in a plan combining a central railway station with an airport, but made as little impact on town planners or leading architects as Tony Garnier's all-embracing *Cité Industrielle* project of 1917. This, *illustrated below as reproduced on apartment walls in Lyon,* was based on zoning districts for residential, industrial, transport, and recreational uses.

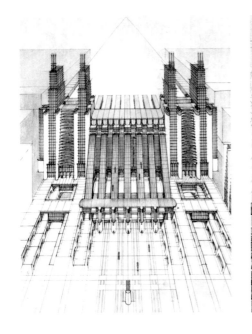

The Union Station, Washington DC, 1908, by Daniel H Burnham, was an integral element in the plan for the city, and a fine example of a classical form in a grandiose style. Meanwhile, Eliel Saarinen was already constructing his most famous building, the Sezessionist-influenced Helsinki Station, 1904–14, with an internal vaulting for which he used exposed concrete.

Perhaps because the railways were one of Mussolini's passions, Milan gained a new station, built between 1925 and 1931 by Ulisse Stacchini, in a style directly contrasting with London's Underground stations of the same period. Here Sir Charles Holden of Adams, Holden & Pearson designed a comprehensive system of stations and signs, which by then had evolved into a continental modern style for brick-built stations based on geometrical elements and with a strong identifying character. In contrast, a new station in the international style was completed in Rome in 1951 by Eugenio Montuori, while London replaced the glorious Victorian Euston Station with a new one in 1963–68, by R L Moorcroft. Similarly, Terry Farrell refurbished Charing Cross Station, 1990–93.

New stations in the Netherlands included one at Eindhoven, 1956, by Van der Gaast, and Central Station, Rotterdam, 1957, by Sybold van Ravesteyn. The Gare Montparnasse in Paris was greatly redeveloped, 1962–69, and new suburban stations were built at Argenteuil, 1970, by R and R Dubrulle, and the Gare de Gringny-Centre, 1974.

It was however Santiago Calatrava who reinvented the railway station with his astonishing free-form Satolas Airport station, Lyon, 1989–94, which established the first link between a European airport and the TGV rail network which is part of the fast-expanding European High Speed Rail System.

Here, the architect has projected a subtle and complex curving fan-shaped canopy to soar as if suspended in space, like an eyelid about to wink. Inside is a vast uncluttered space, quite different to his vaulted cathedral-like Oriente Station, Lisbon, which is part of a huge transport terminus built to serve Expo '98. Both of these stations were newly built with space to spare, and contrast enormously with the highly-acclaimed Lille Europe station, France, 1990–94, by Jean-Marie Duthilleul under the direction of Rem Koolhaas, and the Waterloo International Terminal, London, 1993, by Nicholas Grimshaw, both of which were redeveloped on very cramped existing sites.

As personal and public transport have become an integral part of modern societies, so has provision for them (by way of garaging, parking, bridges, tunnels and junctions) become an essential part of architectural thinking, even though many of these requirements are more engineering than architectural problems. The railways, including metro systems, have become the major mode of transport for the daily commuter, while aircraft shrank

Above: *Union Station, Washington DC, 1908, by Daniel H Burnham*

Above: *Park Royal Underground station, London, 1932, by Charles Holden*
Below: *Gare Montparnasse, Paris, 1962–69, by Baudoin, Cassan, de Marien, Lopez and Saubot. The arched glass entrance was added in 1987*

Above: *the coach terminus entrance to Oriente Station, Lisbon, 1998, by Santiago Calatrava, which was built to link the Expo site with the centre of the city. It combines a coach terminus,* inset left, *with an underground station and the main-line railway station,* inset right, *and a wide range of commercial premises that include banks, restaurants and a supermarket*

the world as more and more aircraft journeys were made each year.

The siting of the major airports of necessity has been on the outskirts of cities, and when starting with a clean sheet of paper, architects have been able to develop many evocative plans, especially as airports have posed entirely new problems. Many of the earlier large airport terminal buildings share a common vast bleakness on soulless and anonymous concourses which seem intended to reflect the wealth and power of the airlines, reducing the passenger to insignificance.

Of the early post-Second World War airports, the terminal building at Lambert Airport, St Louis, 1954–56, by Minoru Yamasaki, appears to have been the inspiration for the far more expressionist TWA Terminal, Kennedy Airport, New York, 1962, by Eero Saarinen. This was designed by Saarinen in 1956 and completed after his death, but the swooping forms created from reinforced concrete shells suggest both the sensuous joy of a bird's

Far left: *Lille Europe station, 1990–94, by Jean-Marie Duthilleul*
Left: *Dulles International Airport, Chantilly, Virginia, 1962–63, by Eero Saarinen*
Below: *Haj air terminal building, Jeddah, Saudi Arabia, 1982, by Skidmore, Owings & Merrill*

flight, and a technology more related to the future than the present. Saarinen also designed the terminal building for Dulles International Airport, Chantilly, Virginia, 1962–63, which serves Washington DC. Its floating roof is supported by cables strung from 32 concrete pylons. Skidmore, Owings & Merrill created the Haj air terminal building, Jeddah, Saudi Arabia, 1982, exclusively for pilgrim traffic at the King Abdul Aziz Airport. Steel masts and hi-tech Teflon fabric were used to create a highly distinctive single structure incorporating tent-like modules, providing shady shelter but plenty of air circulation.

More imaginative airports built during the 1990s include Norman Foster Associates' Stanstead Air Terminal, 1991, a small, friendly and very hi-tech structure. Quite different from any of these is the new terminal building at El Prat airport, Barcelona, opened the following year in time for the Olympics and designed by Richard Bofill's Taller de Arquitecture in an international modern style that echoes the 1930s. Light and spacious inside, it has one of the longest internal axes of any airport.

Kansai International Airport, Osaka Bay, Japan, 1994, by Renzo Piano Workshop, is an airport that seemingly floats on the sea on its own man-made island. The largest construction project of the era, Chep Lap Kok Airport, Hong Kong, was opened in 1998 at a cost of £12 billion and six years' work. The site was originally a range of hills rising from the sea off the south China coast, which was reshaped into a 6 x 3.5 km (4 x 2 miles) artificial island. This massive civil engineering project included provision for 34 km (21 miles) of roads and underwater tunnels, a high-speed train, a massive suspended railway bridge, and a whole new city, Tsung Chung. The airport terminal building, designed by Norman Foster Associates, in plan is shaped like a giant aircraft. A lightweight steel roof is covered in a sequence of shallow vaults supported by the exposed concrete structure.

Above: *El Prat airport, Barcelona, 1988–91, by Ricardo Bofill*
Below: *Chep Lap Kok airport, Hong Kong, by Norman Foster Associates, while under construction in 1998*

Chapter Six

Religious Architecture

VIGOROUS AND EXTENSIVE BUILDING PROGRAMMES had been carried out by the Church throughout Europe since medieval times. The nineteenth-century religious revival coincided with a huge population expansion, providing the impetus for further building in the towns; by the outbreak of the First World War, the religious needs of the population were well provided for. Furthermore, the traditionally conservative Church could see little attraction in the modern architectural style. The result was that new religious buildings were rare in Britain during the first half of the twentieth century. In the middle of the century, the radical questioning of the Church's teaching by its leaders was reflected in a fresher approach to its buildings.

An adventurous church building programme was begun in North America, which resulted in more innovative structures than would have been acceptable in Europe in the early part of the century. Among such buildings were the Unity Temple, Oak Park, Chicago, 1906, by Frank Lloyd Wright, and the Christian Science Church, Berkeley, California, 1912, by Bernard Maybeck. Wright still led the way in America in the 1950s, with the saucer-shaped Annunciation Greek Orthodox Church, Wauwatosa, Wisconsin, 1956, and the Beth Sholom Synagogue, Elkins Park, Philadelphia, 1958–59. These were for different religions and had very different structures, but in Wright's didactic way each is a building which happened to have a religious purpose, rather than being accommodation for a religious meeting place which necessarily has a tangible presence.

As the international modern style was superseded by more inventive and materials-oriented development in the early 1970s, North America gained more interesting religious buildings. For the Garden Grove Community Church, California, 1976–80, Philip Johnson and John Burgee made extensive use of glass and metal to produce a crystal cathedral, a drive-in church of our times.

Similarly in mainland Europe there had been no more exceptional religious building than the *Sagrada Familia* (Church of

Facing page: *the glazed west front of the Anglican Cathedral, Coventry, 1951–62, by Sir Basil Spence; the glass was designed by John Hutton, and depicts angels and Christian figures*

Below: *Garden Grove Community Church, Los Angeles, California, 1976–80, by Philip Johnson and John Burgee, popularly known as the Crystal Cathedral*

Above: *the* Sagrada Familia *(Church of the Holy Family), Barcelona, by Antoni Gaudí, is still incomplete over 100 years after it was begun in 1884*

Below right: *the monastery of Sainte-Marie de la Tourette, Éveux-sur-l'Arbresle, near Lyon, 1953–57, by Le Corbusier*

the Holy Family), Barcelona, begun in 1883 by Antoni Gaudí i Cornet. He had a long life and remained vigorous into old age, but as it remained unfinished upon his death in 1926, his belief that the act of building constituted an act of worship in itself made completion problematic. Currently building continues, in an effort to complete this outstanding building in the near future.

Perhaps the first successful attempt at combining modern materials and structural methods in a European religious building between the wars was the Notre Dame du Raincy, near Paris, 1922–23, by Auguste Perret. This was built in reinforced concrete with a curved concrete vault, yet its interior has a medieval quality, helped to a large extent by the stained glass windows.

In 1955, Le Corbusier completed the Pilgrimage chapel of Notre Dame-du-Haut, Ronchamp, Vosges, France. Begun in 1950 by a vigorous Le Corbusier, this structure has since become one of the most admired, and attacked, religious buildings ever to have been erected. It is a revolutionary and positive statement of modern architecture, that utterly disregards traditional religious practice. The church at Ronchamp is an ambiguous and evocative creation, both exotic and expressive, subjective and rational, that holds a pivotal position in the whole modern movement.

At the same time, and almost as impressive, Le Corbusier's next religious building was the Dominican monastery of Sainte-Marie de la Tourette, Eveux-sur-l'Arbresle, near Lyon, France, 1953–57. Here the several wings of the complex are arranged asymmetrically around a cloistered garden to take full advantage of the site. The standardized cells, reminiscent of his *Unités d'habitation*, are on the upper level to give good views from their balconies. The communal facilities include the library and class-rooms on the entrance level, and the refectory on a lower level.

During the same period in England, Sir Basil Spence's Anglican Cathedral, Coventry, 1951–62, was built. This postwar design retains the remains of the medieval building that was devastated by bombing during the war, within the precinct of the modern building. The resonantly contemporary structure served

Left: *the interior of Brasilia Cathedral, Brazil, 1966–70, by Oscar Niemeyer, showing the building's concrete ribs*

Below: *Anglican Cathedral, Coventry, 1951–62, by Sir Basil Spence, showing Jacob Epstein's sculpture of St Michael overcoming the devil*

as a religious parallel to the Festival of Britain, showcasing the finest creative talents of many important British artists and traditional craftsmen.

Before the cathedral at Coventry had been completed, work had already begun on the yet more controversial modernist Roman Catholic Cathedral, Liverpool, 1960–67, by Sir Frederick Gibberd. The tent-like shape has a central emphasis; the altar is centrally placed and the seating for the congregation arranged in a full circle around it. Sixteen reinforced-concrete pylons thrust through the whole structure, changing in character and direction as they ascend, and terminate in a lofty lantern which contains stained glass designed by John Piper and Patrick Reyntiens. Oscar Niemeyer took a similar approach to Gibberd's with his Roman Catholic Cathedral, Brasilia, 1966–70. He used, far more elegantly, reinforced-concrete ribs to terminate the Crown of Thorns.

Possibly the most original new religious buildings in the closing decades of the twentieth century were those by Tadao Ando and Mario Botta. Ando's Buddhist Hompuku-ji Temple, Awajishima, Japan, 1989–90, is integrated into a pre-existing monastery. The red-pillared hall of the temple has a seated Buddha in the centre. It is situated beneath an oval-shaped lotus basin, and is reached via a long sweeping concrete ramp that ends in a staircase, decending through the centre of the lotus basin. Again, concrete is used extensively, but Ando's skilful use of the modernist geometric vocabulary allows the building's spirituality to be expressed rather than overshadowed.

The Cathedral at Évry, 1988–95, by Mario Botta, was the first cathedral to be built in France for more than 100 years. A 4,800m² (51,667sq ft) reinforced-concrete structure, it is clad both externally and internally in brick. Like the cathedrals of Liverpool and Brasilia it is based on a circular plan, but Évry has an unusual triangular metal frame, which carries its typical Botta roof structure, *illustrated far left*.

Below: *Évry cathedral, Paris, 1988–95, by Mario Botta*

Chapter Seven

Administration and Government

AT THE BEGINNING OF THE TWENTIETH CENTURY, the more developed countries already had strong established central and municipal governments, and much of the new building for government and administrative bodies was in countries in the Middle East, Africa and the Far East.

One example of such new large-scale complexes was that at New Delhi, India, where Edwin Lutyens constructed the last great statement of the British Raj, the Viceroy's Building, between 1912 and 1927. It proved both effective and inventive, an outstanding success that set the pattern for future large-scale government buildings. Another 25 years were to pass before anything similar was attempted, though on a more domestic scale Willem Dudok designed the town hall, Hilversum, the Netherlands, 1929–31. This deeply impressive but simple brick building has a clock tower that emphasises its central position and role in the community. The town hall, Aarhus, Denmark, 1936–42, by Arne Jacobsen and Erik Møller, is the first major public commission in the modern style.

The two most important buildings in the genre at the beginning of the 1950s were equally architecturally distinguished, despite both having been essentially designed by committee; the United Nations headquarters, New York, was completed in 1952, and the UNESCO building, Paris, was constructed 1953–58. Ten architects were selected to submit designs for the UN complex which comprises three buildings: a 39-storey Secretariat block, a conference block and the Assembly. Consultants for the UNESCO building in Paris included Le Corbusier and Walther Gropius, the eventual design being under the control of Marcel Breuer and Pier Luigi Nervi. The building is eight storeys high and Y-shaped in plan with *brise soleil* and tapered *pilotis*, and has a freestanding reinforced-concrete entrance canopy.

Inevitably the planning of any civic building is a long drawn-out process, in consequence of which whole movements in architecture may pass almost unnoticed before construction begins. There were relatively few such buildings commissioned in

Above: *United Nations HQ, New York, 1947–50, by Wallace Harrison and Max Abramovitz*
Below: *the entrance canopy before being raised into position, in front of UNESCO HQ*

Civic buildings of the 1950s

1950–52 civic centre, Säynätsalo, Finland, by Alvar Aalto; planned as the heart of a new town, it is designed around a raised courtyard. It was constructed in red brick and wood with a copper roof, and includes the council chamber, post office, bank, library, shops and offices.

1951–65 Chandigarh, Punjab, by Le Corbusier; a new city, worked on by the architect until his death in 1965. His three major buildings for the new capital of the Punjab were the Courts of Justice *below*, Legislative Assembly, and the Secretariat. Construction was mainly by local semi-skilled labour.

1954–56 The Town Hall, Rødovre, Denmark, by Arne Jacobsen; unashamedly international in style, it consists of two blocks, the smaller of which is a single-storey conference centre with committee rooms.

1955–60 American Embassy, London, by Eero Saarinan; a fussy modern building with an unimaginative interior.

1956–60 Plaza of the Three Powers, Brasilia, by Oscar Niemeyer and Lúcio Costa, *right*; a double multi-storey office block, the Assembly Chamber and the Senate House are arranged on a raised platform, beneath which are the services and further offices.

1957–66 Marin County Government Center, California, by Frank Lloyd Wright (completed after his death); completely lacking in unison, the complex is ugly and out of place.

1958–60 City Hall, Kurashiki, Japan, by Kenzo Tange; Corbusian in style, with exposed shuttering on the main staircase to the principal floor and windows that echo Ronchamp.

1958–63 City Hall, Bat Yam, Israel, by Alfred Neumann with others; a square plan with an upward, stepped-out form.

1958–65 City Hall, Toronto, by Viljo Revell; comprised of two curved office blocks of different heights, shielding the small domed council chamber.

the international style, and postmodernism as a trend was relatively short-lived and localised. Individual architects might try to adapt their work to its context, but evolution and reassessment were more influential in public building works than revolution and radicalism during the last half of the twentieth century.

The real confrontation stemmed from the electronic revolution, which made possible for the first time a dispersed virtual city with a communications network but no fixed centre. Meanwhile in the real world, global industrialisation continued to undermine local traditions, and thus regional identity, structural integrity, indigenous craft, and moral purpose appeared to become lost or at the very least, to be overwhelmed.

This resulted in a re-examination of local traditions, so that developing countries began to reject the glib reproduction of international formulae, seeking out symbolic forms rooted in their pasts that might also express contemporary aspirations. Their hope in doing so was to produce buildings of a timeless character, fusing old with new, local with universal.

In the post-colonial nation of Sri Lanka, the institutions were eclectic mixtures of ancient rituals and modern western ways. The design of its Parliament building, Colombo, 1980, by Geoffrey Bawa, succeeded admirably in these aims. The building, which has wide roofs and deep overhangs, is set on an island, and is approached via a causeway.

Public buildings contemporary with, and contrasting to, Colombo's Parliament include the Ministry of Foreign Affairs, Riyadh, Saudi Arabia, 1979–84, by Hennink Larsen. This combines a modernistic simplicity with regional and pan-Islamic references in its interpretation of the administrative building. The architect has balanced successfully the attraction of westernisation and modernisation against traditional Arabic values. Similarly, and still contemporary with the Bawa building, is the Medhya Pradesh

state Assembly building, Bhopal, 1981–87, by Charles Correa, who borrowed details from nearby Buddhist stupas at Sanchi.

Quite a different approach however was adopted for the Supreme Court, Mexico City, 1987–92, by Teodoro González de León, which represents one of the strongest statements of civic monumentality. The architect has reverted to the idea of a public building on a grand scale, in which the courtrooms themselves were laid out along a pergola-covered internal street or central spine. The overall design incorporates a repetitive geometry, in a construction material of rough bush-hammered concrete with large chips of stone in several colours, intended to be resistant to the corrosive effects of pollution.

Above left: *the interior of the Ministry of Foreign Affairs, Riyadh, Saudi Arabia, 1979–84, by Hennink Larsen*

Above right: *Ministry of Finance, Paris, 1982–88, by Paul Chemetov and Borja Huidobro; a vast viaduct-like building that begins at the Gare de Lyon and terminates on the banks of the River Seine*

Left: *Australian Embassy, Paris, 1973–77, by Harry Seidler*

Right: *Government buildings, the Hague, 1992, which include the general Ministry and the offices of the Prime Minister and cabinet ministers*

Chapter Eight

Office Buildings

EARLY IN THE TWENTIETH CENTURY, there was already enough new technology available to enable high-density office accommodation to be erected on a restricted site. In addition, the typewriter had been in use since 1874 and the electric version became available in 1920; the telephone was patented in 1876; the first working lift was installed in a building in 1889; escalators were available from 1894, and the first fully air-conditioned building, the Larkin building, Buffalo, New York state, by Frank Lloyd Wright, had opened in 1904 although it was demolished in 1949. These essentials of the modern office, in combination with the construction capability, made possible the office skyscraper, from which all aspects of modern business could be conducted with the exception of manufacture. The Woolworth Building, New York, 1913, by Cass Gilbert, was one early example.

Although the Tribune Tower offices opened in 1925 for the *Chicago Tribune* newspaper, Chicago, in a gothic revival design for which John Mead Howells and Raymond Hood had won the competition in 1922, by this time the consensus was that a modern office building or skyscraper should be designed in a modern style. The runner-up in this competition had been Eliel Saarinen, and his elegantly stepped-back vertical design became far more influential.

New offices soon rapidly proliferated right across America. These included a diverse range of buildings by a variety of architects, such as William Van Alen (Chrysler Building, New York, 1928–29); Burnham Brothers (Carbide and Carbon Building, Chicago, 1929); Shreve, Lamb & Harmon (Empire State Building, New York, 1931, constructed with over ten million bricks); George Howe and William Lescaze (Philadelphia Savings Fund Society Building, Philadelphia, 1926–31), and Frank Lloyd Wright (Johnson Wax Administration Building, Racine, Wisconsin, 1936, with additions, 1950).

The international style became firmly established in America during the decade immediately following the Second World War, becoming universally adopted by large corporations

Facing page: La Pacific, which includes the USNER arch, La Défense, Paris, 1990, and in the background, la Tour Societé Général
Below: Chrysler Building, New York, 1928–29, by William Van Alen

Above: *Petronas Towers, Kuala Lumpur, Malaysia, 1991–96, by Cesar Pelli*

Below: *the 52-storey National Westminster Tower, London, 1971–80, by Richard Seifert & Partners, was the tallest building in Europe when completed, at a height of 183 m (600 ft)*

for their office blocks, but from the end of the 1950s there were suggestions that too many designs were uninspiring. One of the earliest significant buildings was the Alcoa Corporation headquarters building, Pittsburgh, Pennsylvania, 1951–53, by Wallace Harrison and Max Abramovitz. It was one of the first examples of metal-faced curtain walling in the United States, having been constructed with pre-stamped aluminium panels in an indented pyramid design, with rows of windows between rows of panels.

Lever House, New York, 1952, by Skidmore, Owings & Merrill was being built at the same time. It has a two-storey horizontal element raised on pilotis and incorporating meeting rooms and a rooftop plaza, and a 21-storey curtain-walled tower. It became the international benchmark for countless office blocks.

Six years later, just a stone's throw away across Park Avenue, the Seagram building was erected. Designed by Mies van der Rohe, this stark rectangle has an austere classical simplicity. The elegant sheer amber glass and bronze-coloured metal columns are supported by the welded frame beneath, to powerful effect.

Alternative architectural approaches were beginning to emerge by the 1960s, as the international style aesthetic lost the appeal of its novelty. Thus by the end of the decade there had been a multiplicity of innovatively styled office buildings, ranging from the Ford Foundation Headquarters, New York, 1963–68, by Kevin Roche and John Dinkeloo, to the same architects' College Life Insurance Company of America, Indianapolis, Indiana, 1967–71. The New York building is in the modern movement manner, twelve storeys high with an enclosed internal garden court to the full height. Three massive piers clad in expensive stone support the delicate glazing to the Fifth Avenue corner, where the two uppermost floors housing the executive offices and dining areas project slightly above the main façade, giving the structure a depth and rhythm unusual for the period. At Indianapolis these architects produced an extraordinarily futuristic trio of truncated pyramids, again supported by huge piers, set in line in the flat landscape.

The variety of office buildings has continued to reflect contemporary design approaches since the 1970s. The World Trade Center, New York, 1972–74 (destroyed in the terrorist attack of 9/11, September 2001) by Minoru Yamasaki, consisted of two closely related towers. The twin Petronas Towers, Kuala Lumpur, Malaysia, 1991–96, by Cesar Pelli, were the tallest office buildings in the world on completion and are joined at the forty-first floor by a 58 m (190 ft) skybridge.

In the same year as the World Trade Center was begun, William Pereira was completing the Transamerica Corporation building, San Francisco, a tall slender pyramid that draws on modern-movement elements to provide an elongated form that is utterly unlike all that surrounds it. The tall slim rectangular block of the John Hancock Tower, Boston, 1969–73, by I M Pei, also utterly dominates its surroundings, to the extent that Trinity church beside it, and the adjacent public library, look out of place. By the following decade, the companies commissioning business premises had become concerned to promote a prestigious image almost to the exclusion of other considerations, and this concern dictated a markedly individualistic approach on the part of the architects. The Trump Tower, New York, 1983, by Swanke Hayden Connell Architects did much to promote such excesses of commercial luxury and public image.

The boom in office buildings across Europe had been marked initially by the Phoenix-Rheinrohr AG administration building, Düsseldorf, 1955–60, by Helmut Hentrich and Hubert Petschnigg; the Pirelli Tower, Milan, 1956–60, by Gio Ponti, and Centre Point, London, 1963–66, by Richard Seifert. Just as in America, the dominance of the rectilinear building form derived from the international style aesthetic had begun to wane by the later 1970s, tempting companies to concentrate on projecting their public images. Such lavish structures followed as the elegant tower, with its supporting concrete core and curtain glass walling, of the National Westminster Tower, London, 1980, by Richard Seifert & Partners. The solid and angular Ransila 1 office building, Lugano, Switzerland, 1981–85, by Mario Botta, has deeply recessed windows and a roof garden with a signature single tree.

Meanwhile, architecture was being turned inside-out. Following the success of the *Centre National d'Art et de Culture Georges-Pompidou* in Paris, Richard Rogers went on to design the Lloyd's of London Building, London, 1979–86, in the style immediately dubbed high-tech. This completely abandoned the whole international style aesthetic, and although initially it was the subject of much vitriol, clearly this new technological approach has been established. Internally the Lloyd's building has a central atrium rising the whole height of the building and crowned by a semi-circular glazed roof, overlooked by the surrounding galleries.

At the same time, Norman Foster's Hong Kong and Shanghai Bank Headquarters had been completed in Hong Kong in 1986, another explicitly high-tech building that has quickly established itself as one of the island's focal points. It is comprised of three linked blocks of differing heights, of which the tallest is 47 storeys. There is a system of external steel trusses that divide the building into five sections and which correspond internally to double-height floors.

Although the global demand exists for yet more prestigious corporate headquarters, nationally companies are downsizing and more people work from home. It is impossible to predict the balance between the different types of buildings that will be required as society itself adapts, but for architects, the future appears far more exciting than ever before, as new materials and techniques are developed to meet these new challenges.

Above: *Sears Tower, Chicago, 1968–74, by Skidmore, Owings & Merrill, built to symbolize Sears Roebuck & Company's position as the largest retailer in the world. The tower soon became a Chicago icon*

Architects and Buildings of the Period

The years of birth and death of each architect are given in parentheses where they are known; page numbers are indexed in bold for text and *italic* for illustrations

Facing page: I M Pei's Louvre pyramid, Paris, 1982–89. Beneath the pyramid is a spectacular entrance hall, accessed from the pyramid by a spiral staircase

D

Maybeck, Bernard Ralph (1862–1957) **119**
An American architect who trained at the École des Beaux Arts, Paris.
Christian Science church, Berkeley, California, 1912 **119**
Mayne, Thom (1944–)
Born in Connecticut, he gained his B Arch from University of Southern California in 1968, and his M Arch from Harvard in 1978. He taught at Harvard, UCLA, Yale and the Southern California Institute of Architecture (SCI-Arc), of which he was a founding member, in 1972. With Michael Rotondi he established Morphosis in Santa Monica, California, in 1979; Rotondi later departed to form his own company.
Kate Mantilini restaurant, Beverly Hills, California, 1986
Cedars Sinai Comprehensive Cancer Care Center, Beverly Hills, California, 1988
Crawford House, Montecito, California, 1987–92
Yuzen Vintage Car Museum, West Hollywood, California, 1992
Meier, Richard Alan (1934–) **35, 62, 66, 97, 99, 102, 103**
Born in Newark, New Jersey; he trained in architecture at Cornell, graduating in 1957 and working in the offices of **Marcel Breuer**, 1960–63, before establishing his own practice in 1963.
In 1969 he arranged the collaborative exhibition *Five Architects* at the Museum of Modern Art, of the work of **Peter Eisenman**, **Michael Graves**, **Charles Gwathmey** and **John Hejduk**, together with his own.
Meier gained his reputation by using modernist white forms, initially on a small scale, for many private houses; larger commissions for offices and museums followed, evolving with more complex plans, rotated axes and layered space, modulated by a masterful use of natural light.
He was awarded the Pritzker Prize in 1984, the Royal Gold Medal in 1988, and became Professor of the American Academy and the Institute of Arts and Letters in 1983. His current practice is that of Richard Meier & Partners at 475 Tenth Avenue, New York, NY 10018.
Smith House, Darien, Connecticut, 1965–67 **62**, *62*
Saltzman House, East Hampton, New York, 1967–69
Weinstein House, Old Westbury, New York, 1969–71 **62**
Twin Parks Northeast housing, New York, 1969–74
Bronx Development Center, New York City, 1970–77
Douglas House, Harbor Springs, Michigan, 1974 **62**
The Atheneum, New Harmony, Indiana, 1975–79 **97**
Museum für Kunsthandwerk, Frankfurt-am-Main, Germany, 1979–84 **97, 99**
High Museum of Art, Atlanta, Georgia, 1980–83 **99**
Bridgeport Center, Bridgeport, Connecticut, 1984–88
Getty Center, Los Angeles, California, 1984–97
City Hall and Library, Den Haag, the Netherlands, 1986–95
Museum of Contemporary Art, Barcelona, Spain, 1987–95 **102**, *102*, **103**
Canal+ HQ, Paris, France, 1988–92
United States Federal Courthouse, Phoenix, Arizona, 1995–2000
Church of the Year 2000, Rome, Italy, 1996–2000
Melnikov, Konstantin Stepanovich (1890–1974) **110**
Educated at the Institute of Art, Sculpture and Architecture, Moscow; he graduated in 1917, then worked in the architectural workshops of the Moscow Soviet and in the architecture department of the People's Commissariat for Education. He was appointed professor at the Higher Artistic Technical Workshops in 1921.
The Saw collective housing, Moscow, 1922
Newspaper offices for *Leningradskaya Pravda*, 1923
Sukharevka Market, Moscow, 1924
Soviet Pavilion, Exposition Internationale des Arts Décoratifs et Industriels Modernes, Paris, 1925

Rusakov Workers' Club, Moscow, 1927–28 **110**, *110*
Melnikov House and studio, Moscow, 1929
Trade Union Theatre, Moscow, 1934
Ministry of Heavy Industry, Moscow, 1934
Mendelsohn, Erich (1887–1953) **9, 10, 57, 58, 59, 108**
Educated at the Technische Hochschule, Berlin-Charlottenburg, and the Technische Universität, München, from which he graduated in 1912. He established his own office in 1918, becoming a founder-member of the *Novembergruppe* and a member of the *Arbeitsrat für Kunst*. He was also a co-founder of the architects' group *Der Ring*. He emigrated to England in 1933, and to the USA in 1941, spending his last years in San Francisco.
Einstein Observatory tower, Potsdam, 1920–21 **9**
Friedrich Steinberg Hermann & Co building, Luckenwalde, 1921
Rudolf Mosse publishing house alterations, 1921–23 (with **Richard Neutra** and Rudolf Henning)
Double villa, Berlin-Charlottenburg, 1922
Weichmann office block, Gleiwitz, 1923
Meyer-Kauffmann textile works, Wüstegiersdorf, 1923
Schocken department store, Stuttgart, 1926–28 (demolished 1960) **10**, *10*
Universum Cinema, Berlin, 1926–28 **108**, *108*
Wohnhausgrundstücksverwertungs-AG community project, Kurfürstendamm, Berlin, 1927–31
Rudolf Mosse pavilion, Pressa Exhibition, Köln, 1928–30
Own house, Grunewald, near Berlin, 1929–30 **57**, *57*
Columbus House, Berlin, 1931–32
De La Warr seaside pavilion, Bexhill-on-Sea, 1934–35 (with **Serge Chermayeff**) **58, 59**, *59*
Schocken Library, Jerusalem, 1934–36
Hadassah Hospital and Medical School, Mount Scopus, Jerusalem, 1934–39
Cohen House, 64 Old Church Street, Chelsea, London, 1936 (with Serge Chermayeff) **58, 59**, *59*
Hospital, Maifa, Palestine, 1937–38
Hebrew University, Jerusalem, 1937–39
Mendini, Alessandro (1931–) **47, 99**
Born in Milan, he gained his doctorate in architecture from the Milan Polytechnic University in 1959.
He was editor of the magazine *Casabella*, 1970–76, of *Modo*, 1977–80, and *Domus*, 1980–85. He created the Domus Academy in 1982. Having been a member of the Archizoom and Superstudio Groups during the 1970s, he collaborated with Studio Alchymia, 1977–91, became the artistic director of Alessi and Swatch, and now practises as Atelier Mendini, Via Sannio 24, 1-20137 Milano, Italy.
Groninger Museum, Groningen, the Netherlands, 1990–94 **47**, *47*, **99**
Meyer and Holler (established *ca* 1907) **108**
Originally a firm constructing houses known as the Milwaukee Building Company, which moved into larger scale commercial work after the First World War. It specialised in a themed, lavishly presented approach and came to dominate theatre building in Hollywood.
Egyptian Theatre, Los Angeles, 1922
Grauman's (now Mann's) Chinese Theatre, Los Angeles, 1927 **108**
Meyer, Hannes (1889–1954) **10, 11**
A Swiss architect who trained in Berlin, and became head of the architecture department at the Bauhaus, 1925–26. He succeeded **Walter Gropius** as director, but was sacked in 1930 for political reasons, after which he worked in Russia before settling in Mexico in 1935.
Mies van der Rohe, Ludwig (1886–1969) **10, 12, 15, 16, 21, 22, 24, 25, 26, 27, 30, 34, 35, 59, 60, 69, 71, 73, 74, 76, 86, 97, 126**
Educated at the Domschule and the Gewerbeschule in Aachen, he worked in the offices of Bruno Paul in Berlin, 1905, and later **Peter Behrens**, 1908–11, at the same time as both **Walter Gropius** and **Le Corbusier**. While there he was put in charge of the design for the German Embassy in St Petersburg. He moved to Den Haag in 1911, before returning to Berlin

in 1913, where he established his own practice. He became a member of the *Novembergruppe* in 1922, and began to use the name of Mies van der Rohe; a year later, together with **van Doesburg**, Lissitzky and Richter, he published the journal *G* (for *Gestaltung*). In 1926 he was appointed vice-president of the Werkbund, and in 1927 as director of the exhibition at Stuttgart-Weißenhof, for which he designed a block of flats. He directed the Dessau Bauhaus from 1930 until it closed in 1932, and before the Second World War emigrated to the USA, where he was director of the department of architecture at the Illinois Institute of Technology, Chicago.
Monument to Karl Liebknecht and Rosa Luxemburg, Berlin, 1926
Weißenhofsiedlung apartments, Stuttgart, 1927 **69**, *69*
Villa Hermann Lange, Krefeld, Germany, 1927–30
German pavilion, international exhibition, Barcelona, 1929
Villa Tugendhat, Brno, Bohemia, 1930
Illinois Institute of Technology, individual campus buildings begun in 1940 and erected until the end of the next decade, including:
  Metal research building, 1943
  Chemistry building, 1945
  Alumni Memorial Hall, 1945
  Crown Hall, 1956 **25**, *25*, **86**
Edith Farnsworth House, Plano, Illinois, 1946–50 **59**, *59*
860–880 Lake Shore Drive apartment houses, Chicago, 1948–51 **21**, *21*, **22**, **69**, **73**, *73*
Promontory apartments, 5530 South Shore Drive, Chicago, 1949 **73**, *73*
Seagram Building, New York City, 1954–58 (with **Philip Johnson**) **27, 126**
Neue Nationalgalerie, Berlin, 1967–68 **30**, *30*, **97**
Miralles, Enric (1955–2000)
Born in Barcelona, where he graduated from the Escuela Técnica Superior de Arquitectura, 1978, and worked with Helio Piñón and Albert Viaplana before forming his partnership with his wife, the architect Carmen Pinós, in 1983. He later practised as Enric Miralles, 52 Avinyo St, E-08002 Barcelona, with the architect Benedetta Tagliabua, his partner and second wife. He has lectured at Columbia University, New York, Harvard, and at the Architectural Association, London.
Plaza de la Estación de Sants, Barcelona, 1981–83 (with Helio Piñón and Albert Viaplana)
Igualada cemetery park, Barcelona, 1985–92
Morella boarding school, Castello, 1986–94
La Mina civic centre, Barcelona, 1987–91
Huesca sports hall, 1988–94
Els Hostalets de Balenya civic centre, Barcelona, 1988–94
Olympic archery ranges, Barcelona, 1989–91
National Training Centre for Rhythmic Gymnastics, Alicante, 1989–93
Unazuki Meditation Centre, Toyama, Japan, 1993–94
Railway station access, Takaoka, Japan, 1993–95
City Hall, Utrecht, the Netherlands, 1998
Scottish Parliament building, Edinburgh, 1999–2001
Moholy-Nagy, László (1895–1946) **12**
Moneo, José Rafael (1937–) **46, 47, 99, 102, 103**
Born in Tudela, Navarra; he graduated from the Escuela Técnica Superior de Arquitectura (ETSA), Madrid, 1961, taught at ETSA in Madrid and Barcelona and was chairman of the Department of Architecture at the Graduate School of Design at Harvard, 1985–90.
National Museum of Roman Art, Mérida, Spain, 1980–86 **99**
San Pablo airport terminal, Seville, Spain, 1989–91
Davis Museum, Wellesley, Massachusetts, 1989–93
Atocha railway station, Madrid, 1991
Miró Foundation, Palma, Majorca, 1992
Thyssen-Bornemisza museum (interior), Madrid, 1992
L'Auditori, Plaça de les Glòries, Barcelona, 1999 **102, 103**
Grand Hyatt Hotel, Potsdamer Platz, Berlin, 2000 **46**, *46*

Government offices, Riyadh, Saudi Arabia, 1978–82

Oud, Jacobus Johannes Pieter (1890–1963) **11, 16, 17**
Educated at the Quellinus School of Applied Arts, Amsterdam, where he worked in the offices of Petrus J H Cuypers before completing his education at the State School of Design, Amsterdam, and the Technical University, Delft. He worked as a freelance architect in Purmerend and Leiden, with **Theo van Doesburg** founding the association *de Sphinx* in 1916. They formed the artists' group *de Stijl* with Piet Mondrian, Vilmos Huszar and Antony Kok, in 1917. Oud was appointed City Planner of Rotterdam in 1918, and in 1954 received an honorary doctorate at the Technical University, Delft.
Terrace house, Scheveningen, 1917 (as *de Stijl*)
Café De Unie, Rotterdam, 1924–25 (restored 1990) **11**, *11*
Workers' housing, Hoek van Holland, 1924–27 **11**, *11*
De Kiefhoek workers' housing development, Rotterdam, 1925
Terrace houses, Weißenhof, Stuttgart, 1927
Blijdorp housing estate, Rotterdam, 1931 **17**, *17*, *18*
Shell Building, Den Haag, 1938–42
Children's convalescent home, Arnhem, 1952–60

P

Panter Hudspith 41
A partnership between Mark Frederick Panter and Simon Hudspith.
Pitcher and Piano pub, Newcastle-upon-Tyne, 1997 **41**, *41*

Pei, Ieoh Ming (1917–) **44, 45, 97, 99, 100, 126, 129**
Born in Canton (now Guangzhou), China; he emigrated to the United States in 1935, gained his B Arch in 1940, his M Arch in 1942 and his doctorate in 1946, both from Harvard. He formed the practice of I M Pei & Associates in 1955 with Henry Nichols Cobb (1926–) and **James Freed**, was awarded the American Institute of Architects Gold Medal in 1979, the Pritzker Prize in 1983 and the Praemium Imperiale, Japan, in 1989.
His current practice is that of Pei Cobb Freed & Partners at 600 Madison Avenue, New York, NY 10022.
National Center for Atmospheric Research, Boulder, Colorado, 1961–67
Federal Aviation Agency (50 air traffic control towers in various locations), 1962–70
John F Kennedy Library, Harvard University, Boston, Massachusetts, 1965–79
National Gallery of Art East Building, Washington DC, 1968–78 **97**
John Hancock Tower, Boston, 1969–73 (designed by Henry Cobb) **126**
Bank of China Tower, Hong Kong, 1982–89
Pyramid, Grand Louvre, Paris, 1983–93 **44**, *44*, *45*, *99*, **100**, *128*, **129**
Bell Tower, Misono, Shiga, Japan, 1990–92
Miho Museum, Kyoto, Japan, 1990–97
Rock and Roll Hall of Fame, Cleveland, Ohio, 1993–95 **100**

Peichl, Gustav (1928–) **100**
Educated at the Staatsgewerbeschule, Mödling, Vienna, the Bundesgewerbeschule, Linz, and the Vienna Academy of Fine Arts; he worked in the offices of Roland Rainer before establishing his own practice in 1956, and taught at the Academy of Fine Arts, Vienna, from 1973.
Atrimschule Krim, Vienna, 1962–63
Dominican convent, Hacking, Austria, 1963–65
Rehabilitation centre, Meidling, Austria, 1965–67
School complex, Diesterweggasse, Vienna, 1969–78
Ground signal station, Aflenz, Austria, 1976–80
Phosphate elimination plant, Berlin-Tegel, 1979–85

Bundeskunsthalle (Federal Art Gallery), Bonn, 1985–92
Kunstforum, Vienna, 1988–92 **100**, *100*

Pelli, Cesar Antonio (1926–) **48, 126**
Born in Tucuman, Argentina; he gained his Dip Arch there in 1949 and emigrated to the USA in 1952, where he attended the University of Illinois, completing his MS Arch in 1954.
He worked in the offices of **Eero Saarinen**, 1954–64, and was the project designer for the TWA terminal at Kennedy Airport, New York City, and the Vivian Beaumont Theatre, New York City. From 1966 until 1977, Pelli was partner in charge of design at Gruen Associates, Los Angeles.
He was appointed Dean of the School of Architecture at Yale in 1977, when he also opened his practice, Cesar Pelli & Associates Inc, 1056 Chapel Street, New Haven, Connecticut, 06510.
Pacific Design Center, Los Angeles, 1975
US Embassy, Tokyo, Japan, 1976
Museum of Modern Art (residential tower and gallery expansion), New York City, 1977
World Financial Center, New York City, 1980–88
Canary Wharf Tower, London, 1987–91
NTT Shinjuku HQ, Tokyo, 1990–95
Sea Hawk Hotel and Resort, Fukuoka, Japan, 1991–95 **48**, *48*
Petronas Twin Towers, Kuala Lumpur, Malaysia, 1991–97 **48**, *48*, **49**, **126**, *126*

Penchreac'h, Georges (1941–) **32**
Les Halles Forum, Paris, 1979 (with **Claude Vasconi**) **32**, *32*

Pereira, William (1926–) **48, 126**
Transamerica Corporation building, San Francisco, 1972 **126**

Perrault, Dominique (1953–) **44, 89, 90**
Born in Clermont-Ferrand, France, he gained his architect's diploma in 1978, followed a year later by a degree in town planning from the École National des Ponts et Chaussées, Paris. He established his own practice in 1981.
ESIEE (engineering school), Marne-la-Vallée, Paris, 1984–87
Hôtel Industriel Jean-Baptiste Berlier, Paris, 1986–90
Bibliothèque Nationale de France, Paris, 1989–96 **44**, *44*, **45**, **89**, **90**, *90*
Olympic velodrome, swimming pool, diving pool, Berlin, 1992–98

Perret, Auguste (1874–1954) **118**
Educated at the École des Beaux-Arts, Paris; he established a construction firm in 1905 with his brothers Gustave and Claude. After the Second World War he was very involved with the reconstruction of Le Havre from 1945–54.
Residential block, rue Franklin, Paris, 1903
Garage, rue de Ponthieu, Paris, 1905
Théâtre des Champs-Élysées, Paris, 1911–13 (from a concept of **Henry van de Velde**)
Esders clothing workshop, Paris, 1919
Notre-Dame du Raincy church, Paris, 1922–23 **118**
Musée des Travaux Publics, Paris, 1937
Church of St Joseph, Le Havre, 1954

Piacentini, Marcello (1881–1960) **106**
Palazzo dello Sport, Rome, 1958–60 **106**, *106*

Piano, Renzo (1937–) **32, 37, 38, 39, 45, 46, 93, 97, 99, 115**
Born into a builder's family in Genoa, Italy, he graduated from the school of architecture at Milan Polytechnic in 1964, where his design tutor had been Franco Albini.
From 1965 to 1970 he worked in Philadelphia with **Louis I Kahn**, and in London with Z S Makowsky. He collaborated with **Richard Rogers** from 1971 (Piano and Rogers), and with Peter Rice from 1977 (Atelier Piano & Rice).
His many awards and acknowledgments include the Legion d'Honneur, Paris, 1985, the RIBA Royal Gold Medal for Architecture, England, 1989, the American Academy of Arts and Letters Honorary Fellowship, 1994, the Erasmus Prize, Amsterdam, and Praemium

Imperiale, Japan, 1995, and most recently the Pritzker Prize, in 1998. His current offices are Renzo Piano Building Workshop, at via P P Rubens 29, 16158 Genova, Italy, and at 34 rue des Archives, F-75004 Paris.
Centre National d'Art et de Culture Georges-Pompidou, Paris, 1971–77 (with Richard Rogers) **32**, *32*, **37**, *92*, **93**, **97**, **98**, **127**
B & B-Italia offices, Novedrate, near Como, Italy, 1973
De Menil Collection museum, Houston, Texas, 1981–86 **37**, **38**, *38*, **99**
Cité International plan (multiplex cinema, hotel and casino), Lyon, France, 1985–98
San Nicola football stadium, Bari, Italy, 1987–89
Bercy2 shopping centre, Paris, France, 1987–90
Kansai International Airport Terminal, Osaka Bay, Japan, 1988–94 **38**, **39**, *39*, **115**
IRCAM office extensions, Paris, 1990
Jean-Marie Tjibaou cultural centre, Nouméa, New Caledonia, 1991–98
Potsdamer Platz area for Daimler Benz, Berlin, 1992–2000 (includes the musical theatre, casino, housing and IMAX theatre, plus the Debis HQ, completed 1997) **45**, *45*, **46**, *46*
Church for Padre Pio, San Giovanni Rotondo, Foggia, Italy, 1994–95
Museum of Science and Technology, Amsterdam, the Netherlands, 1997

Poelzig, Hans (1869–1936) **9, 69, 93, 94**
He graduated from the Technische Hochschule, Berlin-Charlottenburg, 1899, then worked for the Preußisches Staatsbauamt. Appointed professor at the Kunstgewerbeschule, Breslau (now Wrocław, Poland), in 1900, he was promoted to principal, 1903–16, after which he became professor and municipal architect of Dresden. From 1920 he taught at the Prussian Academy of Arts, and from 1924 also at the Technische Hochschule, Berlin-Charlottenburg.
Municipal water tower, Posen, Germany (now Poznan, Poland) 1911 **9**
Chemical factory, Luban, Germany (now Poland), 1911–12 **9**, *9*
Exhibition structure, centennial exhibition, Breslau (Wrocław, Poland), 1913
Großes Schauspielhaus, Berlin, 1919 **93**, **94**, *94*
Capitol shop and cinema, Berlin, 1924
Berlin Trade Fair, 1929 (with Martin Wagner)
Broadcasting House, Berlin, 1930 (with Martin Wagner)
IG Farben building (now Poelzig-Bau), Frankfurt-am-Main, 1930

Polshek, James Stewart (1930–)
Born in Akron, Ohio, he attended Case Western Reserve University, Cleveland, Ohio, 1951, and gained his M Arch from Yale, 1955.
He established his own practice of Polshek Partnership, 320 West 13th Street, New York, NY 10014-1278 in 1963, and was appointed Dean of the Graduate School of Architecture, Columbia University, New York, 1972–87.
Seaman's Church Institute, New York City, 1991
Center for the Arts Theatre, Yerba Buena Gardens, San Francisco, 1993
Inventure Place, Akron, Ohio, 1993–95
Ministry of Construction building, Chambéry-le-Haut, France, 1994
Rose Center for Earth and Space, American Museum of Natural History, New York City, 2001

Ponti, Gio (1891–1979) **127**
He studied architecture at the Politecnico, Milan, 1918–21, returning to teach there from 1936 to 1961.
Montecatini office building, Milan, 1936–51
Pirelli Tower, Milan, 1956–60 (with **Pier Luigi Nervi**) **127**
Baghdad Government Offices, 1958 (with Antonio Fornaroli)
Banca Antoniana, Padua, Italy, 1962 (with Antonio Fornaroli and Alberto Rosselli)
Government Secretariat, Islamabad, Pakistan, 1964–68 (with Fornaroli and Alberto Rosselli)
Museum of Modern Art façades, Denver, Colorado, 1972

Portzamparc, Christian de (1944–) **36**, **37**, **44**, **45**, **100**, **101**
Born in Casablanca, he studied at the École des Beaux Arts, Paris, 1962–69. He won the competition for the Cité de la Musique project in 1984 and was awarded the Pritzker Prize in 1994, a year before it was completed.
He participated in the Euralille project, with a tower over the Lille-Europe railway station.
Water Tower, Marne-la-Vallée, Paris, 1971–74
Hautes Formes apartments, Paris, 1975–79
Cité de la Musique, 1984–95 **44**, *44*, **45**, **100**, **101**, *101*
Crédit Lyonnais towers, Euralille complex, Lille, France, 1997 (with **Claude Vasconi**) *36*, **37**
Palais des Congrès (additions), Paris, 1999

Powell and Moya
A J Philip Powell (1921–) and John Hidalgo Moya (1920–94) made contributions to three of the colleges of Oxford University: Brasenose, Christchurch and Wolfson.
Churchill Gardens housing estate, Pimlico, London, 1946
Skylon, Festival of Britain, London, 1951 (destroyed) **23**, *23*
Mayfield School, Putney, London, 1956
Festival Theatre, Chichester, 1962

Predock, Antoine (1936–) **100**
Born in Lebanon, Missouri, he was educated at the University of New Mexico and Columbia University, gaining his B Arch in 1962. He established his own practice in 1967.
Nalson Fine Arts Center, Arizona State University, Tempe, Arizona, 1986–89
Zuber House, Phoenix, Arizona, 1986–89
American Heritage Center, Laramie, Wyoming, 1987–93 **100**, *100*
Civic Arts Plaza, Thousand Oaks, California, 1989–94
Hotel Santa Fe, Euro Disney, Marne-la-Vallée, Paris, 1990–92
Ventona Vista elementary school, Tucson, Arizona, 1992–94

Prince, Bart (1947–) **66**
Mead-Penhall House, Albuquerque, New Mexico, 1992–93 **66**
Hight House, Mendocino County, California, 1994–95 **66**, *66*

Prix, Wolf D (1942–) *see* **Coop Himmelblau**

Q

Quintana, Màrius see **Galí, Beth**

R

Raymond, Antonin (1888–1976)
He studied at the University of Prague, 1906–10, then emigrated to the USA and changed his name from Rajman. He worked for **Cass Gilbert** in New York City, 1910–12, and for **Frank Lloyd Wright** in both Chicago and Taliesin, 1912–17, and in Tokyo, 1919–20. He remained in Japan in private practice, 1923–37, when he returned to the USA for a ten-year period before going back to Japan once again.
Rising Sun Petroleum Company offices, Yokohama, 1926
Fukui House, Atami Bay, Tokyo, 1933–35
Kawasaki House, Tokyo, 1934
Ford Motor Company plant and offices, Tsurumi, 1934
Golconde dormitory, Aurobindo Ashram, Pondicherry, 1936–48
Defence housing, Bethlehem, Pennsylvania, 1940
Readers Digest building, Tokyo, 1947–49 (demolished 1964)
Midtown art galleries, New York City, 1948
Nanzan University, Nagoya, Japan, 1960–66
International School, Nagoya, Japan, 1966
Pan-Pacific Forum, University of Hawaii, Honolulu, 1966–69

Reidy, Affonso Eduardo (1900–64)
He studied at the Escola Nacional de Belas Artes, Rio de Janeiro, where he later taught (1930–31). He was appointed Professor of Architecture in 1931 at the Federal University, returning there in 1954 to be Professor of

Urban Planning. Between 1936 and 1943, he worked for the Ministry of Education and Health, Rio de Janeiro, along with **Le Corbusier** and others.
Pedregulho housing estate, Rio de Janeiro, 1947–52
Communal theatre, Rio de Janeiro, 1950
Museum of Modern Art, Rio de Janeiro, 1954–59

Revell, Viljo (1910–64) **122**
City Hall, Toronto, 1958–65 **122**

Rewal, Raj (1934–) **81**, **82**
Asian Games housing, New Delhi, 1980–82 **81**, **82**, *82*
Campus, National Institute of Immunology, New Delhi, 1988
CIET buildings, New Delhi, 1991
World Bank, New Delhi, 1993
Library, Parliament building, New Delhi, 1995

Rietveld, Gerrit Thomas (1888–1964) **11**, **52**, **53**, **58**, **60**, **87**
He established himself as a cabinet maker, setting up in practice in 1917, later joining de Stijl and remaining a member until its dissolution in 1931. In addition, he was a founder member of CIAM in1928. He is credited with having produced the only successful interpretation of de Stijl architectural principles in his design of the Schröder House, Utrecht.
Schröder House, Utrecht, 1923–24 **11**, **52**, *52*, **58**
Van der Vuurst de Vries house, Utrecht, 1927–28 **58**, *58*
Terrace house, Werkbund Exhibition, Vienna, 1932
Vreeburg cinema, Utrecht, 1936
Dutch pavilion, Venice Biennale, 1954
Sculpture pavilion, Sonsbeck Park, Arnhem, 1954 (rebuilt in Otterlo, the Netherlands, 1965)
Academy of Industrial Design and Applied Art, Amsterdam, 1956–58 **87**
School, Badhoevedorp, the Netherlands, 1958–65
Van Dantzig House, Santpoort, the Netherlands, 1959–60
Van Gogh Museum, Amsterdam, 1963–72 (completed by J van Tricht)

Roche, Kevin Eamonn (1922–) **97**, **126**
Gained his BA in architecture from the National University of Ireland, Dublin, where he was born; then he worked in the offices of Michael Scott and Partners and **Maxwell Fry**, London. From 1948 he was working in the USA for the Illinois Institute of Technology and in the planning office of the United Nations; then in the planning department of **Eero Saarinen** and Associates, Bloomfield Hills, Michigan, 1950–61. After Saarinen's death in 1961, Roche worked on the completion of the former's major projects with **John Dinkeloo**, and in 1966 they changed the name of the company to Kevin Roche John Dinkeloo and Associates.
Oakland Museum, California, 1961–68 **97**
Ford Foundation building, New York City, 1963–68 **126**
Fine Arts Center, University of Massachusetts, Amherst, 1964–74
Knights of Columbus HQ, New Haven, Connecticut, 1965–69
Aetna Life and Casualty computer building, Hartford, Connecticut, 1966–72
College Life Insurance Company of America HQ, Indianapolis, Indiana, 1967–71 **126**
Metropolitan Museum of Art (extensions), New York City, 1967–85
General Foods Corporation, Rye, New York, 1977–82
Leo Burnett building, Chicago, 1989 *6*, *7*

Rogers, Richard (1933–) **32**, **37**, **46**, **47**, **93**, **97**, **105**, **127**
He studied at the Architectural Association School, London and at Yale University, New Haven, Connecticut, under **Serge Chermayeff**. In 1963 he formed Team 4 with his wife, Su, and **Norman** and Wendy **Foster**. He taught at the Architectural Association School, Cambridge, and in London, during 1967, and from 1969 he lectured in the USA at Yale University, Massachusetts Institute of

Technology, and Princeton University.
With **Renzo Piano** he won the competition for the Centre National d'Art et de Culture Georges-Pompidou, Paris, 1971, but in 1977 this collaboration with Piano ended when he created the Richard Rogers Partnership in London. He was knighted in 1991, and ennobled, as Lord Rogers of Riverside, in 1996.
Reliance Control Factory, Swindon, Wiltshire, 1967 (as Team 4)
Own house, Wimbledon, 1968–69
Centre National d'Art et de Culture Georges-Pompidou, Paris, 1971–77 (with Renzo Piano) **32**, *32*, **37**, *92*, **93**, **97**, **98**, **127**
PA Technology laboratory, Cambridge, 1975–83
Fleetguard factory and warehouse, Quimper, France, 1978
Lloyds of London HQ, London, 1979–86 **37**, *37*, **127**
Inmos microprocessor factory, Newport, Wales, 1982
PA Technology laboratories, Princeton, New Jersey, 1984–86
Channel 4 television HQ, London, 1990–94
Tribunal de Grand Instance, Bordeaux, 1993–98
Office buildings, Potsdamer Platz, Berlin, 1994–97 **46**, *46*
Housing, Potsdamer Platz, Berlin, 1994–2000
Millennium Dome, London, 1999 **105**, *105*

Rossi, Aldo (1931–97) **78**, **79**, **80**, **89**, **97**
Born in Milan, he entered the Milan Polytechnic in 1949 but worked for the magazine Casabella-Continuità before graduating in 1954. He became editor of Casabella-Continuità in 1964, was appointed professor at Milan Polytechnic in 1965, and published his highly-regarded book, Architecture and the City, in 1966.
He became professor at the Federal Polytechnic of Zürich in 1972 and of the University of Venice in 1973. He was awarded the Pritzker Prize in 1990.
Gallaratese apartments, Milan, 1969–76 **78**, **79**, *79*
Cemetery, San Cataldo, Módena, Italy, 1971–90
Elementary school, Fagnano Olona, Italy, 1974–77 **89**
Teatro del Mondo, Venice, 1979 **97**
Südliche Friedrichstadt housing complex, Berlin, Germany, 1981–88 **80**
Centro Torri shopping centre, Parma, Italy, 1985–88
Il Palazzo hotel, Fukuoka, Japan, 1989
Modern Art Museum, Vassivière, Limousin, France, 1988–90
Office tower, Mexico City, 1994–98

Roth, Alfred (1903–) and **Emil** (1893–1980)
Doldertal apartments, Zürich, Switzerland, 1934–36 (with **Marcel Breuer**) **68**, *68*

Rotondi, Michael (1949–)
Born in Los Angeles, he gained his B Arch from the Southern California Institute of Architecture (SCI-Arc) in 1973, later becoming director of the Graduate Design Faculty, 1976–87, and then director of SCI-Arc. He was a founding principal of **Morphosis** with **Thom Mayne**, leaving that practice in 1991 to create his own.
Nicola restaurant, Los Angeles, 1993

Rudolph, Paul Marvin (1918–97)
Educated at the Alabama Polytechnic Institute, Auburn, and at Harvard University, Cambridge, Massachusetts, he established his own practice in 1952. He was appointed chairman of the school of architecture, Yale University, New Haven, Connecticut, in 1958.
Mary Cooper Jewett Arts Center, Wellesley College, Wellesley, Massachusetts, 1955–58
High school, Sarasota, Florida, 1958–59
Art and architecture building, Yale University, New Haven, Connecticut, 1958–64
Milam House, Jacksonville, Florida, 1960–62
State Service Center, Boston, Massachusetts, 1967–72

S

Saarinen, Eero (1910–61) **26**, **28**, **76**, **87**, **106**, **114**, **115**, **121**, **122**

His family emigrated from Finland to the United States in 1923, but Eero first studied sculpture at the Académie de la Grande Chaumière, Paris, then architecture at Yale University, New Haven, Connecticut. After graduating he worked for his father's practice in Ann Arbor, Michigan. He established his own practice in 1950, in Birmingham, Alabama.
Jefferson National Expansion Memorial, St Louis, Missouri, 1948 (built 1963)
General Motors Technical Center, Warren, Michigan, 1949–56
Kresge auditorium, Institute of Technology, Cambridge, Massachusetts, 1950–55 **87**
Chapel of Concordia Senior College, Institute of Technology, Cambridge, Massachusetts, 1953–55
David S Ingalls ice hockey rink, Yale University, New Haven, Connecticut, 1953–58 **106**
Trans World Airlines terminal, John F Kennedy Airport, New York City, 1956–62 **114**
American Embassy, London, 1957–60 **120**, **121**, **122**
John Deere & Co HQ, Moline, Illinois, 1957–63
Dulles International Airport, Chantilly, Virginia, 1962–63 **28**, *28*, **115**, *115*
Saarinen, Eliel (1873–1950) **13**, **125**
He is widely regarded as being a leading exponent of the Art Deco style.
Helsinki Station, 1904–14 **113**
Safdie, Moshe (1938–) **28**, **29**
Habitat '67, Expo '67, Montréal, 1967 (with David, Barrott Boulva) **28**, **29**, *29*
Sant'Elia, Antonio (1888–1916) **112**
La Città Nuova, 1913–14 **112**, *112*
Sartoris, Alberto (1901–98)
Born in Turin, this son of a sculptor was educated in Geneva at the École des Beaux Arts. Graduating in 1919, he returned to Italy and worked in the offices of Raimondo D'Aronco and Annibale Rigotti until founding his own practice in 1926. In 1928, he was chosen by **Le Corbusier** as the Italian representative at the Congrès Internationaux d'Architecture Moderne (CIAM). He belonged to the *Movimento Italiano per l'Architettura Razionale*, and was the initiator of functionalism in Italy. He was made editor of the periodical *La Città futurista* in 1929, contributed to the Cercle et Carré exhibition in Paris in 1930, and published *Gli elementi dell' architettura Funzionale* in 1932, with a foreword by Le Corbusier. In 1946, he became Professor of Art History at the University of Lausanne.
Pavilion, Turin Exhibition, 1928
Notre-Dame du Phare church and religious centre, 1931
Notre-Dame du Bon Conseil, Lourtier, Switzerland, 1932
Morand-Pasteur House, Saillon Valais, Switzerland 1934–35
Scarpa, Carlo (1906–78)
He was educated at the Academy of Fine Arts, Venice, and in 1926 was appointed assistant to Guido Cirilli at the Instituto Universitario di Architettura. In 1962 he was made associate professor for interior design, and a director in 1972, teaching there until 1977.
Muranesi Cappellin & Co glassworks shop interior, Florence, 1928
Paul Klee pavilion, Venice Biennale, 1948
Art publications pavilion, Venice Biennale, 1950
Museo Correr, Venice, 1953–60 (alterations)
La Foscari Palace, Venice, 1954–56
Galeria degli Uffizi, Florence, 1954–56 (six rooms, with Ignazio Gardella and Giovanni Michelucci)
Gipsoteca Canoviana, Possagno, Treviso, Italy, 1955–57 (extensions)
Veritti House, Udine, Italy, 1955–61
Olivetti showrooms, Venice, 1957–58
Castelvecchio Museum, Verona, 1964 (alterations)
Brion-Vega cemetery, San Vito d'Altivole, Treviso, Italy, 1969–78
Banco Popolare di Verona, 1980 (completed by Arrigo Rudi)
Scharoun, Hans Bernhard (1893–1972) **7**, **69**, **70**, **74**, **96**

Educated at the Technische Hochschule, Berlin, 1912–14, he worked as an architect for the Militärbaukommando on the East Prussia Reconstruction Programme, 1915–18, after which he became acting director of town planning, Insterburg. He practised as an independent architect from 1919, but in the offices of Paul Kruchen until 1925, where he directed several rebuilding projects. He was a member of the *Gläserne Kette* group. He taught at the State Academy, Breslau (now Wroclaw, Poland), 1925–32, and became a member of *Der Ring* association of architects.
Between 1929–30 he was director of the Siemensstadt housing development, Berlin. After the Second World War he was appointed director of the Bau-und Wohnungswesen (building and housing department), Berlin, where he was responsible for the Collective Plan reconstruction programme, 1946. He was professor of town planning at the Technische Universität, Berlin, 1940–58, and director of the Institat für Bauwesen der Deutschen Akademie der Wissenschafte, Berlin, 1947–50.
Kamswyken district development (Die Bunte Reihe), 1920
Apartment building, Werkbund Exhibition, Breslau (now Wroclaw, Poland), 1929
Apartment block, Siemensstadt Estate, near Berlin, 1929–30 **70**, *70*
Apartment block, Jungfernheideweg, Berlin, 1930
Apartment block, Mäckeritzstraße, Berlin, 1930
Schminke House, Löbau, Germany, 1933
Mattern House, Bornim, Potsdam, Germany, 1934
Baensch House, Berlin-Spandau, 1935
Moll House, Berlin, 1937
Geschwister-Scholl-Gymnasium, Lünen, 1956–62
Berlin Philharmonic Hall, Berlin, 1956–63 **96**, *96*
Romeo and Juliet apartment blocks, Stuttgart, Germany, 1957–59 **74**, *74*, **75**
City theatre, Wolfsburg, Germany, 1965–73
Berlin State library, 1967–78 **96**
Schipporeit Heinrich Associates 76
Lake Point Tower, Chicago, 1968 **76**, *76*
Schindler, Rudolf Michael (1887–1953) **13**, **55**
He studied under **Otto Wagner** at the Akademie der bildenden Künste, Vienna, 1910–13, and worked in the offices of Hans Mayr and Theodor Mayer, 1911–14, after which he moved to Chicago to work for Henry A Ottenheimer, Stern and Reichert, and from 1917 in the offices of **Frank Lloyd Wright** where he was primarily employed on the Tokyo Imperial Hotel project. He moved to Los Angeles in 1920 to establish his own practice, forming the Architectural Group for Industry and Commerce (AGIC) in 1926 with **Richard Neutra**. During the 1930s he built several houses and apartment houses in the Los Angeles area and participated in exhibitions. His *Space Architecture* article was published in 1934, and reprinted the following year in the *Los Angeles Times*.
Schindler / Chase House, Hollywood, California, 1921–22
El Pueblo Ribera Court holiday community, La Jolla, California, 1923–25
Packard House, South Pasadena, California, 1924
Lovell Beach House, Newport, California, 1925–26 **55**
C H Wolfe House, Avalon, Catalina Island, 1928–29
Lowes House, Eagle Rock, Los Angeles, 1932
Bethlehem Baptist Church, Los Angeles, 1944
Schneider, Till (1959–) and **Schumacher, Michael** (1957–)
Till Schneider was educated at the University of Kaiserslautern and gained his diploma from the Technische Hochschule, Darmstadt.
Michael Schumacher attended the same university, and a postgraduate course with Schneider at Staatliche Hochschule für Bildende Künste, Städelschule, Frankfurt-am-Main, before working in the offices of **Norman Foster**,

London, and Braun & Schlockerman, Frankfurt-am-Main.
Schneider + Schumacher was formed in 1988.
J Walter Thompson offices, Frankfurt-am-Main, 1994–95
KPMG (Deutsche Treuhandgesellschaft) offices, Leipzig, 1997
Schuchov, Vladimir Grigorevich (1853–1939)
He studied engineering at the Polytechnic of Moscow, 1871–76, and worked in St Petersburg where he was concerned with the planning of locomotive sheds. Between 1878–80 he worked on pipelines in Baku, following a commission from Alexander V Bovi. On his return to Moscow he became chief engineer in Bovi's office, developing a new water supply system for the city in 1886. He constructed bridges for the railways and developed large-roof construction, publishing *The Roofing Bond*, 1897.
Petrovskij Arcade, Moscow, 1893
GUM department store, Moscow, 1894
Adziogol lighthouse, Chersson, Black Sea, 1911 (demolished)
Transmitting tower, Comintern Radio Station Shabolovka, Moscow, 1919–22
Schultes, Axel (1943–)
Born in Dresden, Germany, he graduated from the Technical University of Berlin in 1969. He worked with Dietrich Bangert, Bernd Jansen and Stefen Scholz in the BJSS partnership from 1974 to 1991, establishing his own practice, Axel Schultes, Lützowplatz 7, D-10785 Berlin, Germany, in 1992.
Kunstmuseum, Bonn, 1985–92
Büropark am Welfenplatz, Hannover, 1993
Baumschulenweg Crematorium, Berlin, 1997–98
Schweitzer, Josh (1953–)
Born in Cincinnati, Ohio, he gained his BA from Pitzer College, Claremont, California, and an M Arch from the University of Kansas, 1980.
He worked in the offices of Spence + Webster, London, PBNA in Kansas City, and **Frank O Gehry** in Santa Monica, before establishing his own practice, Schweitzer BIM.
The Monument, Joshua Tree, California, 1987–90
California Chicken Café, Los Angeles, 1992
Venue restaurant, Kansas City, 1993
Big Life Sports Bar, Fukuoka, Japan, 1995
Scott, Chesterton and Shepherd 94
The firm was headed by Elizabeth Scott (1898–1972), the grand-daughter of George Gilbert Scott, and the first woman in England known to have designed a public space such as the Royal Shakespeare Theatre (later renamed).
Shakespeare Memorial Theatre (Royal Shakespeare Theatre), Stratford-upon-Avon, Warwickshire, 1929 **94**, *94*
Seidler, Harry (1923–)
Born in Austria, he studied in Vienna, 1932–38, Manitoba, Canada, 1941–44, and at Harvard University, 1945–46. He worked with **Marcel Breuer**, 1946–48, and **Oscar Niemeyer**, 1948, before emigrating to Australia.
Rose Seidler House, Turramurra, Sydney, 1948
Rose House, Turramurra, Sydney, 1950
Australia Square redevelopment, Sydney, 1961–67 (with **Pier Luigi Nervi** as engineer)
Commonwealth Trade Group office, Canberra, 1970–75
Australian Embassy, Paris, 1973–77 **123**, *123*
Riverside Centre, Brisbane, 1983–86
Seifert, Richard (1910–2001) **27**, **127**
Centre Point office block, London, 1966 **27**, *27*, **127**
NatWest Tower (now International Financial Centre), London, 1971–80 **126**, *126*, **127**
Printing House Square newspaper offices, London, 1974
Semper, Gottfried (1803–79) **9**
The most important German architect of the mid-nineteenth century.
Sert, José Luis (1902–83) **60**, **87**, **88**, **97**
A Spanish architect who worked for **Le Corbusier**, 1929–32. He emigrated to America in 1939, and succeeded **Walter Gropius** at Harvard, 1953–69.